SCRUPLES

A Journaling Workbook for Personal & Group Development

Antonio Gully

Copyright Page

ISBN 978-0-9975042-4-8

Library of Congress Control Number 2019905444

Editing by Sierra Dean

Book Design Antonio Gully

Printed and bound in the United States of America

First Printing June 2019

To order additional copies of this book, contact the author:

Antonio Gully

antonio.j.gully@gmail.com

https://squareup.com/store/AntonioGully

Objective

This workbook is designed to facilitate critical thinking and provide guidance for those aged 13 years + with a progressive perspective. With communication gaps between generations growing, Scruples serves to mend those gaps utilizing positive, healthy, and collaborative strategies. Additionally, this multifaceted tool enhances self-awareness. When used to supplement existing personal or organizational development, participants will benefit from strengthened intellectual and character building skills.

Select activities are designed to be completed with an adult who consistently demonstrates patience, resourcefulness, and understanding. Scruples is a robust resource with activities that help improve self -confidence, family bonds, and healthy relationships.

Upon completion, workbooks should be stored in a secure place and reviewed every 2-5 years. Its probable that responses will change. Jot new thoughts and ideas on a blank sheet and staple to the page. Be sure to add the date.

TOGETHER, LET'S BRING OUT THE BEST IN OURSELVES AND OTHERS.

Benefits of Journaling

Builds IQ and cognitive functioning
Organizes cluttered thoughts
Relieves Stress
Assist in Achieving goals
Builds Emotional Intelligence
Sparks Creativity
Builds Confidence & communication skills

General Steps to Personal Mastery & Improvement

I

Admit that you don't know everything and need help. Be honest with yourself and the process.

II

Pinpoint the exact areas you desire to develop. Be absolute. Be concise.

III

Willingness to seek knowledge and assistance. Network/Listen/Research/Learn/Review/Understand, until desired knowledge is gathered.

III

Devise a plan of action with gathered information.

IV

Implement/Execute the plan fully.

V

Reflect on outcome.

VI

Reward yourself for accomplishing the goal.

VII

Repeat

(*Be sure you fully understand yours and others mistakes before repeating)

Powerful Traits For Successful Youth Development

Resourcefulness: This trait allows you to effectively find and use knowledge and emotion to achieve a goal.

Creativity: Engages and frees the mind in a way that enables a person to absorb or release knowledge and energy through alternative ways of thinking. This trait is helpful in all areas of life.

Empathy: One must have the ability to understand all sides and be able to put oneself in another persons' shoes.

Curiosity: This trait is what triggers one to want to learn more and find the unknown.

Sociability: It always serves best to be able to adapt, communicate, and move effectively in any setting or circle. This trait of versatility can help you quickly maximize your network.

Bounce Back: The ability to comeback stronger after a failure or setback. There are no loses, only lessons. Learn from yourself and others mistakes to comeback stronger.

Self Awareness/Oneness: One must have the ability to understand their effect on the world around them and vice versa.

Integrity : Your word is bond, one must have the ability to build and maintain healthy trustworthy relationships with those in and out of their environment.

✓ When addressing a task, instead of saying, "I have to do" etc. Find the positive or purpose of the task using words such as, "I get the chance to do" or "I get the opportunity to do" etc. Simply training yourself to switch those few words, can have extreme positive affects on ones life.

Universal Scruples of the Strong and Righteous

Universe, Heaven, and Earth

Commit to something greater than One's Self.
Recognize the existence and be committed to a supreme being, principle, and transcendent purpose to one existence.

Self

Self Respect and love, but with humanity, self discipline, and acceptance of personal responsibility.
Respect, understand, nurture, and care for one's self .
Do not exalt oneself or over indulge.
Show humility and avoid gluttony, greed, or other forms of selfishness.
Act in accordance with one's conscience and take full responsibility for one's behavior.

Other Humans

Respect and Care for others.
Recognize the connectedness between all people.
Serve humankind and be helpful for individuals.
Be caring, respectful, compassionate, tolerant, and forgiving to others.
Do not hurt others. (do not murder, lie, steal, cheat, and abuse)
Care for other living and deceased things.
Care for the environment.

Understanding and Overcoming Conflict

Understanding that everybody has their own beliefs, biases, and insecurities.

Some of these beliefs have been built over a lifetime, which are only backed by opinion, folklore, experience, and assumptions. When faced with this conflict, it's ok to 'agree to disagree'.

Understanding the "us vs them" mentality

Group bonds and common interest build loyalty and strong relationships. When individual conflict or suspicion arises from an outside group, inaccurate understandings of each others views tend to foster. Opposing positions can come off as more extreme than they actually are. If you're experiencing conflict as a group or on your own, you can overcome the propensity to criticize and vilify the other side by looking for and highlighting a common identity or goal.

Understanding Antagonistic traits

Be sure to watch out for those who attempt to threat, yell, discredit, name-call, hurt, or arouse you in a negative way during a conflict. They want a reaction that can give them leverage or make you feel, how they feel. Don't stoop to their level.

Look beneath the surface to identify deeper issues

Ask yourself, what can make a person feel or act this way? What are they trying to accomplish with their behavior? Sometimes it's best to just listen. Often the deeper issue will come out on its own.

Separate the things you find sacred and the things you don't care about

Ask yourself, are they or myself in conflict to save image or pride? Whats the objective? Differentiate the things you find sacred and pseudo-sacred to save time, relationships, and stress.

The 7 Learning Styles

Understanding these learning styles can not only help you master your ability to intake knowledge and information but also assist in building strong communication skills.

Visual (Spatial):

Prefers using images, pictures, and spatial understanding.

Ways To Enhance Retention

- Use charts, graphs, maps, diagrams, time lines and info-graphics.
- Implement digital tools & technology to assist learning.
- Replace words with colors and images.

Aural (Auditory-Musical):

Prefers using music, rhythm, and sound.

Ways To Enhance Retention

- Participate in discussions & debates.
- Read Aloud
- Use jingles or rhymes to remember new material.

Verbal (Linguistic):

Prefers using words, both in speech and writing.

Ways To Enhance Retention

- Take thorough notes, reread and rewrite your notes. Make summaries of your notes.
- Create lists with key words and phrases to help you remember concepts. Use acronym mnemonics to assist in recall.
- Go over old tests.

The 7 Learning Styles

Physical (Kinesthetic):

Prefers using their body, hands and sense of touch.

Ways To Enhance Retention			
	Hands-on lessons.	Review and recite notes while doing other physical activities.	Use role playing or mime games to act out subject material.

Logical (Mathematical):

Prefers using logic, reasoning and systems.

Ways To Enhance Retention			
	Try to understand the key concepts behind lessons.	Pull key info from notes such as stats and facts to create lists.	Turn material & lessons into strategic mind games.

Social (Interpersonal):

Prefers to learn in groups or with others.

Ways To Enhance Retention				
	Seek cooperative learning settings.	Use role playing to enhance learning.	Teach others what you have learned.	Learn about others perspectives.

Solitary (Intrapersonal):

Prefers to work alone and use self-study.

Ways To Enhance Retention			
	Find a quiet but comfortable place to study alone.	Find connections between what you've learned and new information.	Keep a learning journal or log to track personal learning goals.

Method to the Madness

GOAL SETTING & EXECUTION

It is important to break down your goals and task into manageable, obtainable sections. Your short term goals should prepare you for your ultimate goal. Understand few big goals are accomplished in short periods of time. Be patient, be diligent, be motivated and work your process.

Goals For The Year

3 Year Goals

5 Year Goals

10 Year Goals

GOAL TRACKER

PERSONAL GOAL

GOAL	REWARD/BENEFIT OF COMPLETION	ACTION STEPS	DD	REVIEW

RELATIONSHIP/FAMILY GOAL

GOAL	REWARD/BENEFIT OF COMPLETION	ACTION STEPS	DD	REVIEW

COMMUNITY GOAL

GOAL	REWARD/BENEFIT OF COMPLETION	ACTION STEPS	DD	REVIEW

*DD= DUE DATE

GOAL TRACKER

PERSONAL GOAL

GOAL	REWARD/BENEFIT OF COMPLETION	ACTION STEPS	DD	REVIEW

RELATIONSHIP/FAMILY GOAL

GOAL	REWARD/BENEFIT OF COMPLETION	ACTION STEPS	DD	REVIEW

COMMUNITY GOAL

GOAL	REWARD/BENEFIT OF COMPLETION	ACTION STEPS	DD	REVIEW

*DD= DUE DATE

GOAL TRACKER

PERSONAL GOAL

GOAL	REWARD/BENEFIT OF COMPLETION	ACTION STEPS	DD	REVIEW

RELATIONSHIP/FAMILY GOAL

GOAL	REWARD/BENEFIT OF COMPLETION	ACTION STEPS	DD	REVIEW

COMMUNITY GOAL

GOAL	REWARD/BENEFIT OF COMPLETION	ACTION STEPS	DD	REVIEW

*DD= DUE DATE

Table of Contents

Daily Diet Check

Everything around you is food, rather it be for your phyisical, mental, and /or spiritual. Just like a bad or toxic food diet, other things you consume from your environment, friends, family etc. can also have negative longterm effects, This is the same for a positive diet/ environment, having longterm positive effects. Consciously or unconsciously the envirnment around us influences our behaviours and understanding of the world we live in. We can have better control of the positive and negative effects of our daily diet by holding the things we consume and the environment around us to a positive standard.

Physical

Food intake, liquid intake, workout plan, drug use.

No physical activity, with harmful diet including over eating and over consumption of unnatural sugars, ingredients, & substances.

30-60 minutes of Physical activity or exercise, with healthy diet including proper eating habits and consumption of natural foods, ingredients, & substances.

Mental

What kind of things do you read? What type of conversations do you engage in with the people you spend the most time with? Where do you spend most of your time? What kind of music do you listen to? What media do you use for information? What shows and movies do you watch most?

Not reading or learning anything new. Reading, discusing, and/or sharing false news, people, gossip, hate & or lies. Overly Listening to or influenced by music, or media that promotes violence, unhealthy habits, or the degradition of self, others, or Earth.

Learning & applying new & useful information. Reading, discussing, &/or sharing helpful ideas, positive unbiased informative news, etc. Listening to Positive, uplifting, motivating music, or media that promotes healthy habits or the elevation of self, others, or Earth.

Spiritual

What type of people do you connect with? What type of environments do you put yourself in? What guides your daily beliefs, mindset and what influences it?

Consistently in environments that dont serve your purpose. Environments and people that speak to your lower self. In company of negative people, places, or things that guide your beliefs. Those with ill intentions.

Consistently in environments that serve your purpose. Environments & people that speak to your higher self, & push you to be the best version of yourself. In company of positive, people, places, or things that guide your beliefs in a healthy direction. Those with good intentions.

LEVEL I

L1-TASK CHALLENGE

Create an affirmation to speak to yourself in times of stress or insecurity. List your vices and scratch them off as you work to eliminate them.

Friendly greet/honk/wave at people outside during your commutes

MY INNERSTANDING OFME

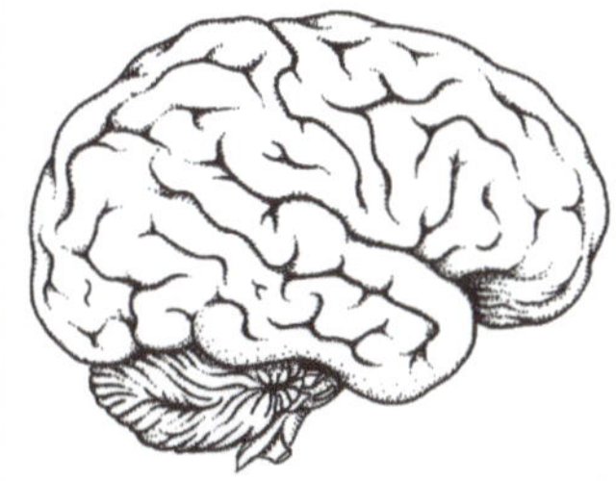

DESCRIBE YOURSELF USING NOTHING BUT ADJECTIVES.

Impetuous: acting without thinking, impulsively.

PSYCH/QUOTES

Always be confident. People admire it, mostly because most people don't have it.

MY INNERSTANDING OFME

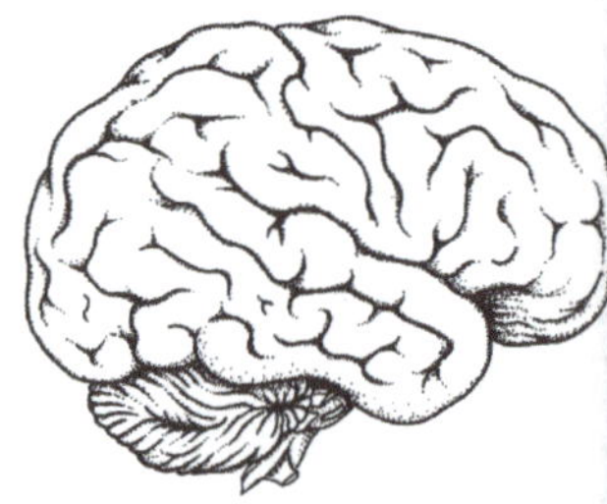

WHAT ARE THE TRAITS YOU LOOK FOR IN A FRIEND? WHY?

Fortitude: courage in pain or adversity.

NOTES

MY INNERSTANDING OFME

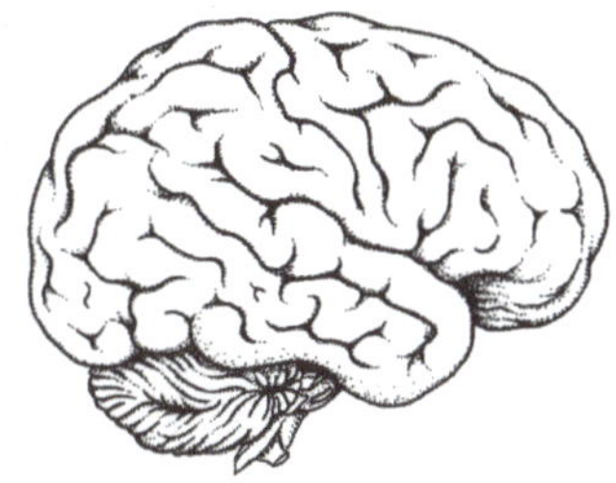

HOW DOES COMMITMENT MAKE YOU FEEL? WHY DO YOU BELIEVE IT MAKES YOU FEEL THAT WAY?

Proclivity: a natural inclination or tendency to act a certain way

PSYCH/QUOTES

Enthusiasm is contagious. Infect those around you with it whenever you want someone to express the same excitement as you.

MY INNERSTANDING OFME

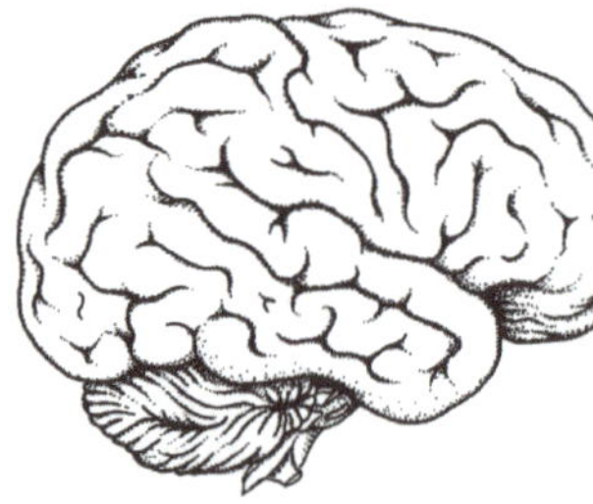

TO WHAT EXTENT ARE YOU WILLING TO GO TO KEEP YOUR WORD? ARE THOSE ACTIONS AGAINST YOUR CHARACTER?

CONGLOMERATE: A NUMBER OF DIFFERENT THINGS OR PARTS THAT ARE PUT OR GROUPED TOGETHER TO FORM A WHOLE BUT REMAIN DISTINCT ENTITIES.

NOTES

MY INNERSTANDING OFME

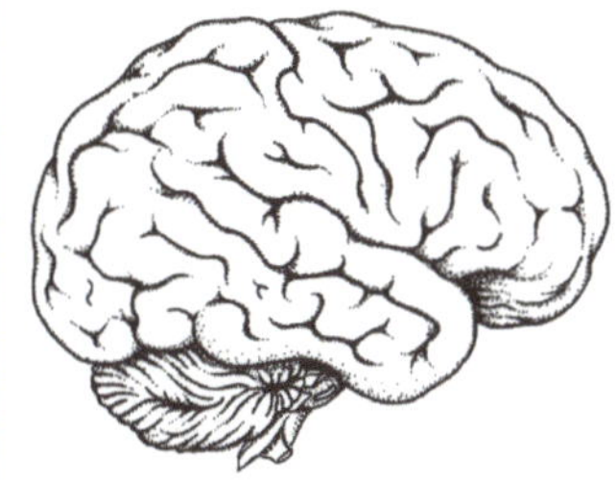

WHAT TYPE OF PEOPLE BRING OUT THE BEST IN YOU?

Querulous: full of complaints.

PSYCH/QUOTES

The universe bares no ill to you, bare no ill to it.

MY INNERSTANDING OFME

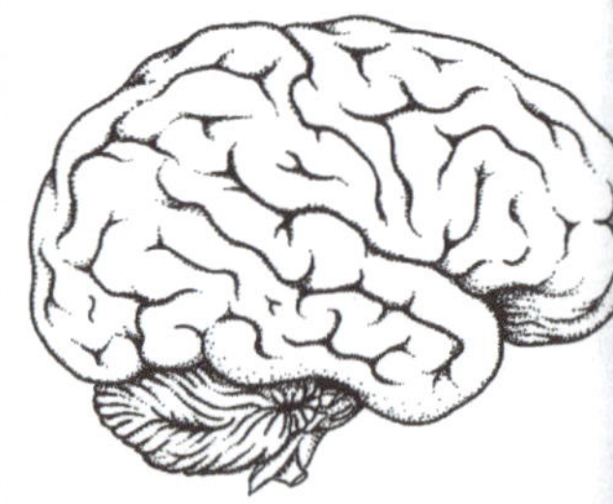

Reconciliation: the restoration of friendly relations.

WHAT ARE SOME TALENTS AND SKILLS YOU WISH YOU HAD? DESCRIBE HOW YOU WOULD GO ABOUT GAINING THOSE SKILLS. EXPLAIN HOW YOU WOULD USE THEM.

NOTES

MY INNERSTANDING OFME

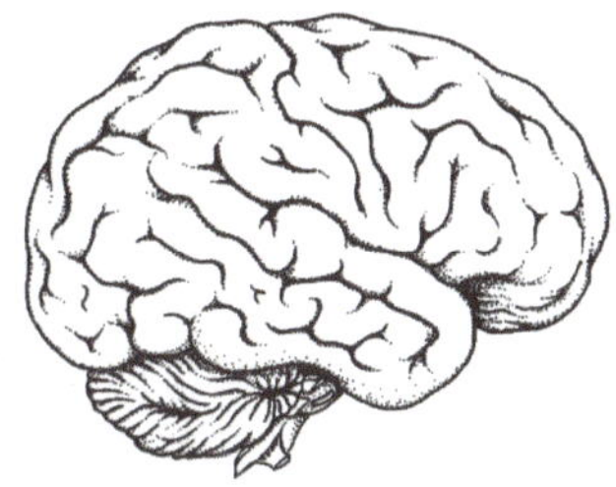

WHAT ARE THE PROS AND CONS OF WORKING TOGETHER AND ALONE. WHICH DO YOU PREFER? WHY?

Phlegmatic: not easily upset, excited, or angered.

PSYCH/QUOTES

Admit when you're wrong. Ask when you need help. You don't know everything, you can't do everything. You're human. Just be the best human you can be.

MY INNERSTANDING OFME

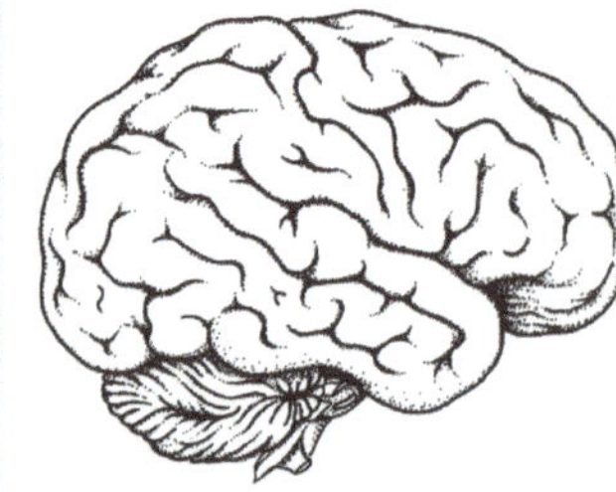

DESCRIBE A TIME YOU QUIT AND EXPLAIN HOW YOU FEEL TODAY ABOUT YOUR DECISION. WHAT WOULD YOU DO DIFFERENT IF YOU COULD.

Cognitive Dissonance: the state of having inconsistent thoughts, beliefs, or attitudes, especially as relating to behavioral decisions and attitude change.

NOTES

MY INNERSTANDING OFME

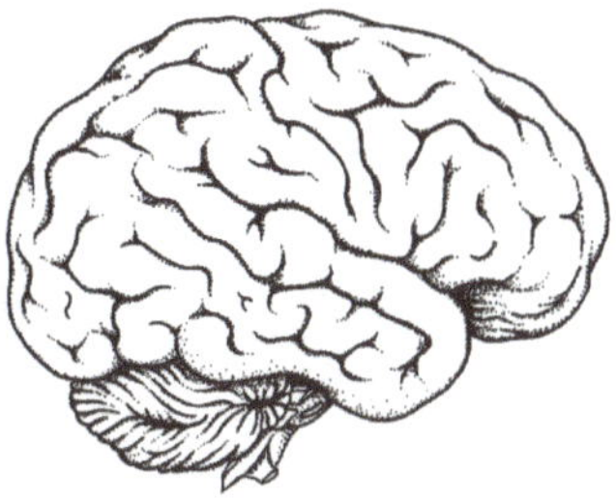

WHAT MAKES YOU A GOOD PERSON/FRIEND?

Clairvoyant: the ability to see beyond the range of ordinary observation.

PSYCH/QUOTES

Ask questions, people love talking about themselves.

MY INNERSTANDING OFME

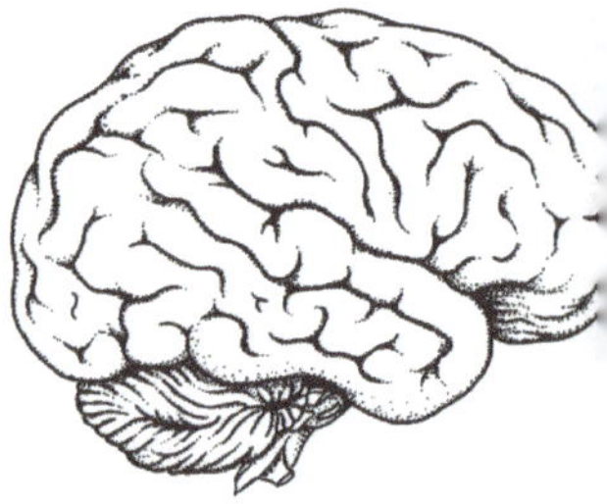

WHAT DO YOU WANT TO BE RESPECTED FOR?

Utopia:
a place or state of things in which everything is perfect, according to ones own standards

NOTES

INTERACTIVE BUILDING ACTIVITY

ACTIVITY

Ask 3 friends to describe what they truly think/feel about you? Ask 2 strangers? Explain how the responses made you feel.

Write an elevator speech that describes yourself and your goals.

On a blank sheet of paper, draw a picture of you at work.

Describe a time when you were praised by your peers. Describe a time when you were praised by superiors. What did you do to warrant the praise? How did the praise make you feel?

SCENERIOS

You see someone who is new to the job/school. During your lunch break you see them sitting alone looking sad. What do you do?

ASK AN ELDER

What does perception mean to you? Personal and Outer. (Ask 3 trusted elders)

Do you have any regrets? What are they?

If you could make the universal rules to street fighting, what would they be? How could you resolve the conflict and keep all parties safe?

LEVEL II

L2-TASK CHALLENGE

In one day, give 20 different people a thoughtful nice compliment.

Create a monthly budget for fun activities.

Think of something you need. Figure out the price and begin saving your $1 bills until you can buy it.

MY INNERSTANDING OFME

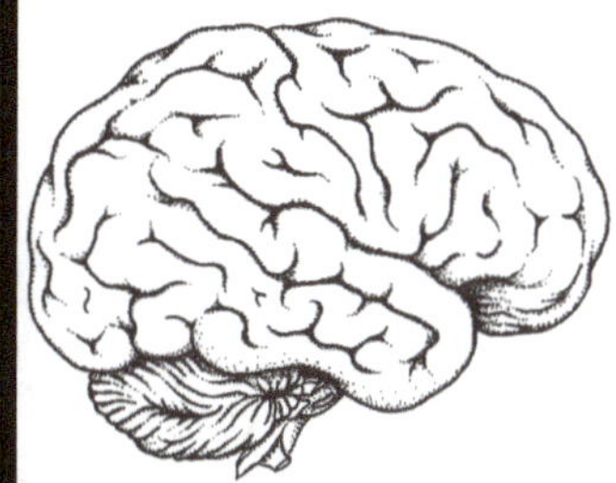

WHAT IMAGE DO YOU WANT TO PORTRAY TO YOUTH? ELDERS?

Conscience: an inner feeling or voice viewed as acting as a guide to the rightness or wrongness of one's behavior.

PSYCH/QUOTES

Reward positive behavior. Give compliments and thanks when someone does something you like. Positive reinforcement motivates one to repeat desired actions.

MY INNERSTANDING OF ME

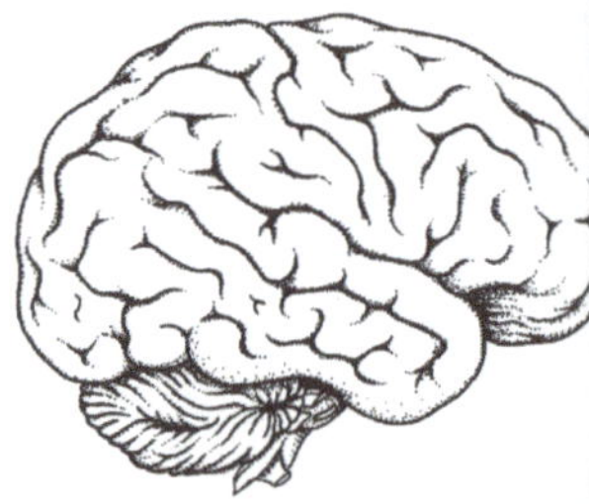

HOW DOES MUSIC/ART MAKE YOU FEEL?
DESCRIBE YOUR FAVORITE LYRICS OR ARTWORK.
LIST YOUR TOP ARTIST AND WHY.

Tranquility: the quality or state of being peaceful, calm, at ease.

NOTES

MY INNERSTANDING OFME

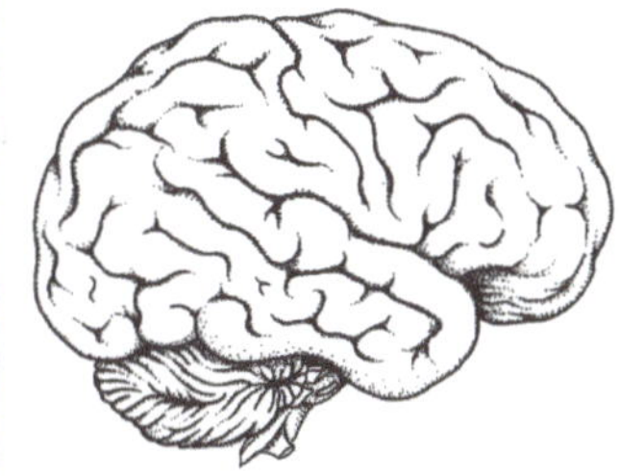

WRITE DOWN HOW YOU WOULD WANT PEOPLE TO THINK AND SPEAK ABOUT YOU WHEN YOU'RE NOT AROUND. HOW IMPORTANT IS THEIR PERCEPTION OF YOU?

Cultural Assimilation: the process in which a minority group or culture comes to resemble those of a dominant group.

PSYCH/QUOTES

Don't be Cocky, but exude importance.

MY INNERSTANDING OFME

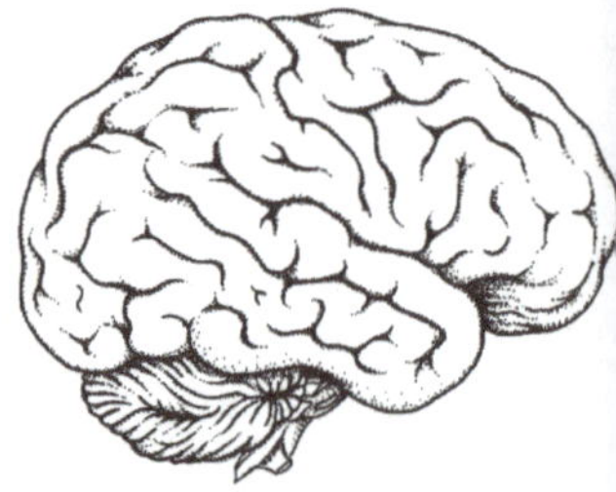

WHAT IS THE BIGGEST CHALLENGE OF BEING A PARENT? SON? DAUGHTER?

Diplomatic: having or showing an ability to deal with a variety of people in a sensitive and effective way.

NOTES

MY INNERSTANDING OF ME

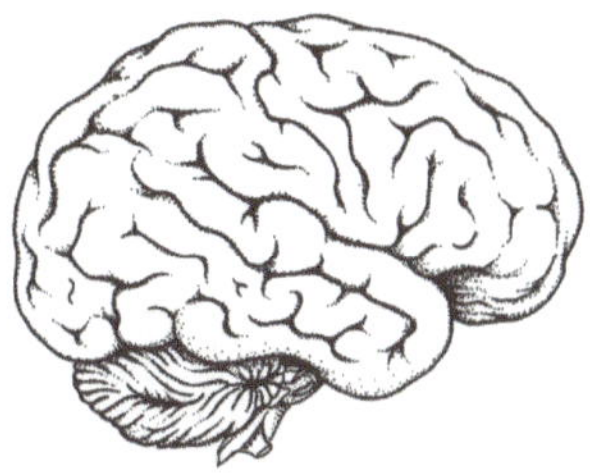

WHAT WAS YOUR BIGGEST OBSTACLE/CHALLENGE GROWING UP? HOW DID YOU OVERCOME IT?

Timid: displaying a lack of courage or confidence.

PSYCH/QUOTES

Never look like you're rushing but always walk with a purpose. Chin up, chest out, and eyes forward.

MY INNERSTANDING OFME

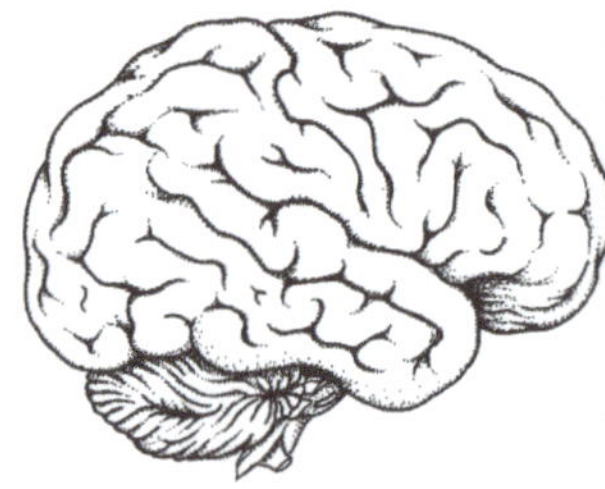

WHAT IS YOUR RESPONSE TO PHYSICAL CONFLICT?

Mentality: the characteristic attitude of mind or way of thinking of a person or group.

NOTES

MY INNERSTANDING OF ME

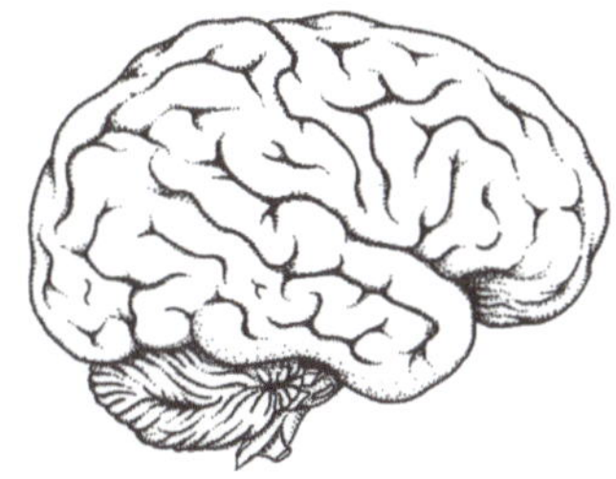

Procrastination: the action of delaying or postponing something.

HAVE YOU EVER HAD TO DEAL WITH ABUSE? HOW DID IT AFFECT YOU? EXPLAIN. WHAT SHOULD BE THE CONSEQUENCES OF ABUSE?

NOTES

MY INNERSTANDING OFME

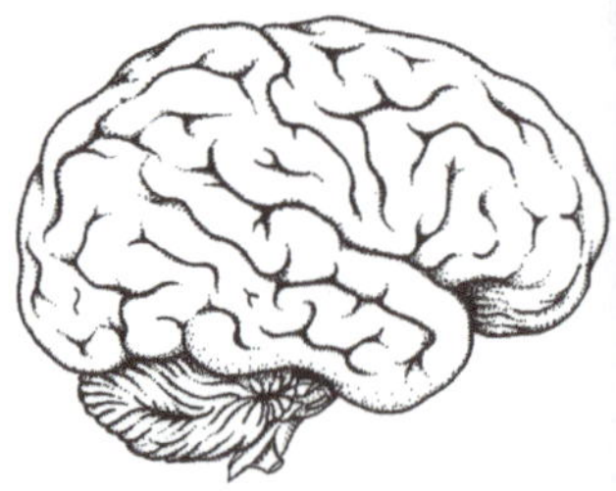

WHAT IS YOUR RESPONSE TO INTERNAL CONFLICT?

Aptitude: a natural ability to do something.

PSYCH/QUOTES

When meeting new people, find commonalities.

MY INNERSTANDING OFME

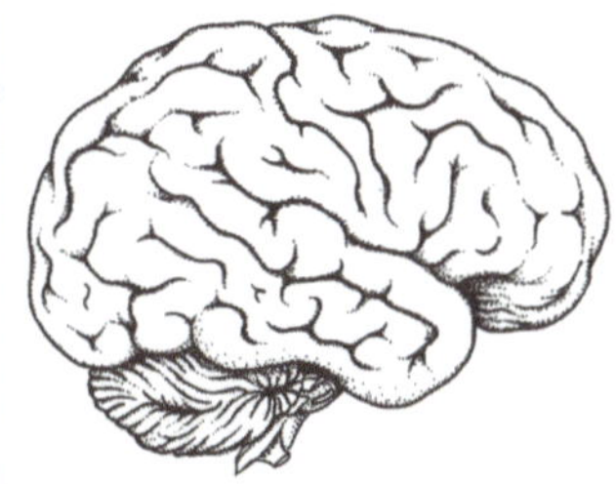

WHAT DOES MANHOOD/ WOMANHOOD MEAN TO YOU?

Impervious: Unable to be affected by. Immune and invulnerable

PSYCH /QUOTES

It's said that pride and fear are the cancers to understanding and peace.

MY INNERSTANDING OFME

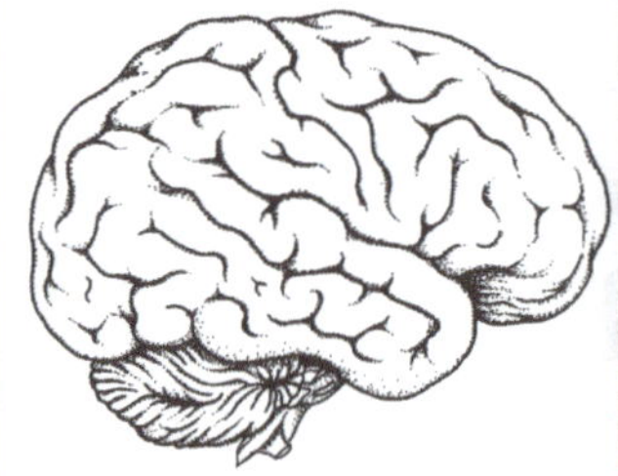

WHAT QUALITIES OR CHARACTERISTICS CAN A PERSON YOUR AGE EXUDE TO SHOW ADVANCED SOCIAL, FINANCIAL, AND EMOTIONAL DEVELOPMENT? WHAT ABOUT ARRESTED DEVELOPMENT?

Empathy: the ability to understand & share the feelings of another.

PSYCH/QUOTES

Excuses are tools of incompetence, used to build monuments of nothingness, those who excel in excuses, seldom excel in anything else, but excuses.

INTERACTIVE BUILDING ACTIVITY

ACTIVITY

Write a letter to your future self describing who you want to be and something important you want to know when you get that age.

List the most influential books you've read to date. What are some things you've learned from them?

With a group of friends, research the top 10 industries that will be dominate in the next 5-10 years. Discuss how you all can enter and prosper in those industries collectively or separately.

Move your mouse to the opposite side of your computer. Switching every week for a month.

SCENERIOS

During a test, you notice a person behind you copying all of your answers. What do you do?

ASK AN ELDER

Describe what a true friend is to you. (*Ask 3 trusted elders)

Describe the type of mentor you wish you had growing up.

What do you believe the next 10-15 years will be like for your community?

Find your Lane

Answer the questions in the large part of the circle, then list the similarities where the circles meet. In the center, list the things that combine them all. Next, answer the "Think Ahead" questions on the next page.

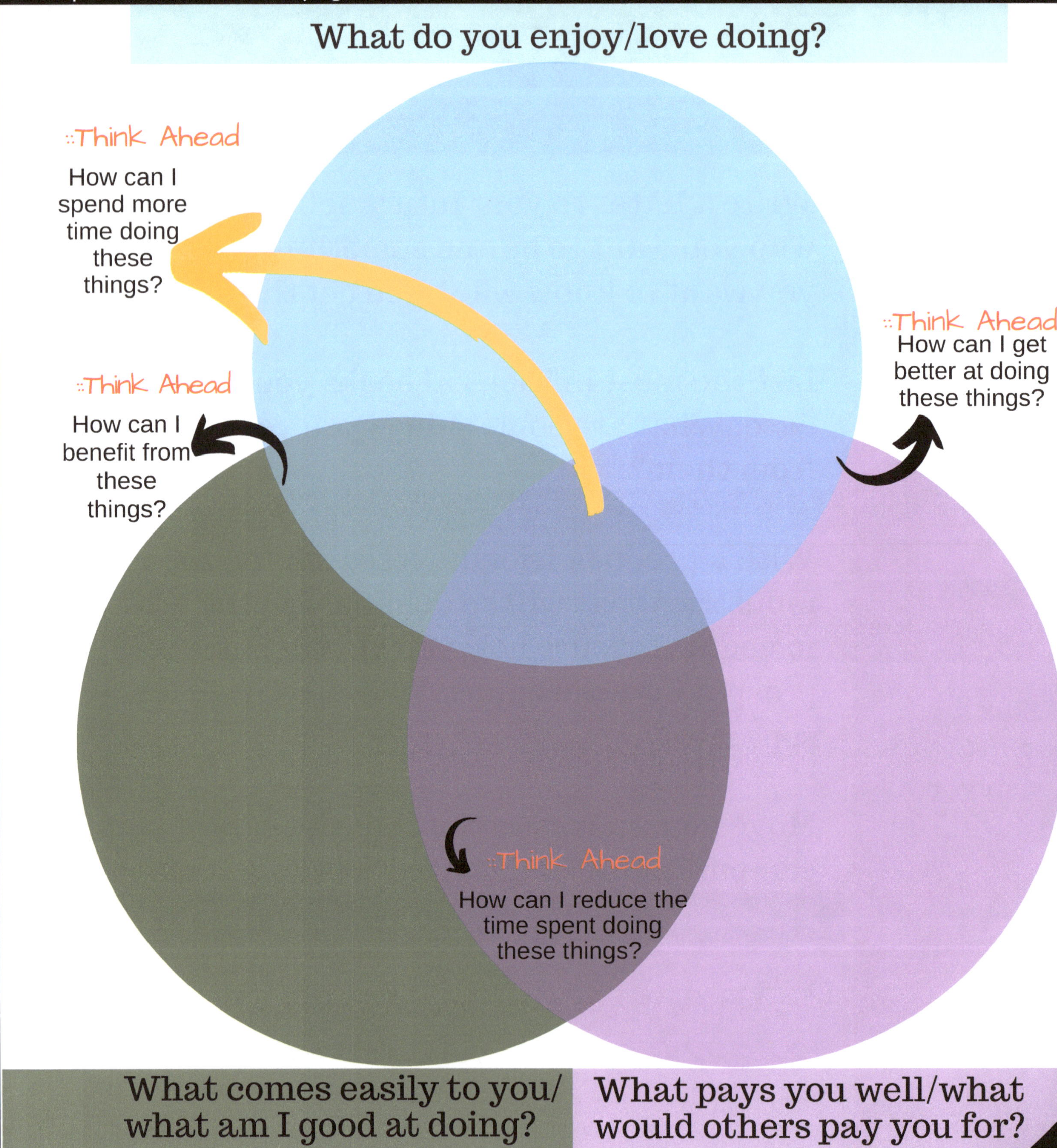

::Think Ahead

From the the center section: How can you spend more time doing these things?

How can I get better at doing these things?

How can I reduce the time spent doing these things?

How can I benefit from these things?

LEVEL III

L3-TASK CHALLENGE

Send a motivational text to friends you feel that need it. Give motivational words to strangers/people you see looking down.

What is one thing you can do to improve yourself today? Write about what you will do, then write a second reflection tomorrow about your experience.

How do you work with deadlines? Finish early or wait until last minute? Rate your ability to focus and complete a task correctly (1-10). Ask a business partner or teacher to rate you.

MY INNERSTANDING OFME

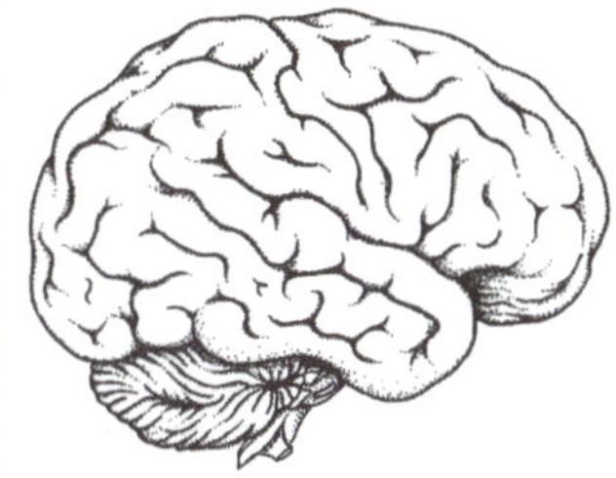

HOW SHOULD PEOPLE YOU DON'T LIKE BE TREATED? WHY?

Perfectionist: one who refuses to accept any standard short of perfection.

PSYCH/QUOTES

When giving negative feedback, begin with 2 positives, then state the negative, followed by another positive. This keeps the persons confidence high and motivates them to correct the negative.

MY INNERSTANDING OFME

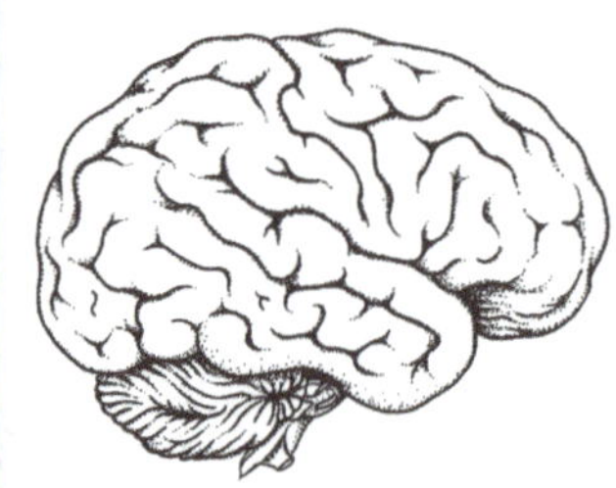

DO YOU HATE?? WHAT DO YOU HATE? WHY?

Paradigm Shift: an important change that occurs when the usual way of thinking about or doing something is replaced by a new and different way.

NOTES

MY INNERSTANDING OFME

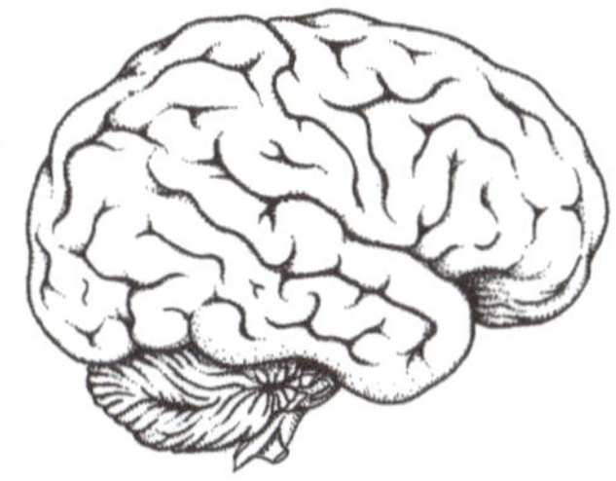

WHAT IS THE BEST COMPLIMENT YOU'VE EVER RECEIVED?
WHAT'S YOUR MOST DESIRED COMPLIMENT? PUBLIC? PRIVATE?

Equity: the quality of being upstanding, fair, and impartial.

PSYCH/QUOTES

Listen and provide validation during conversations. Head nods and rephrasing show that you understand, care, and listen.

MY INNERSTANDING OF ME

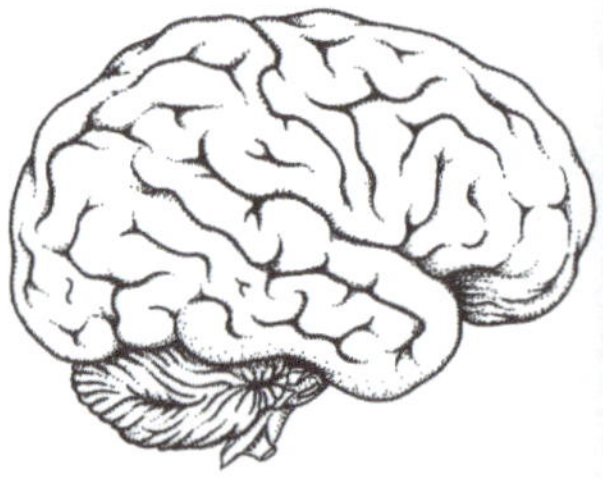

ARE YOU GIVING? WHAT DO YOU GIVE? TO OTHERS, TO YOURSELF?

Indoctrination: the process of teaching a person or group to accept a set of beliefs uncritically.

NOTES

MY INNERSTANDING OFME

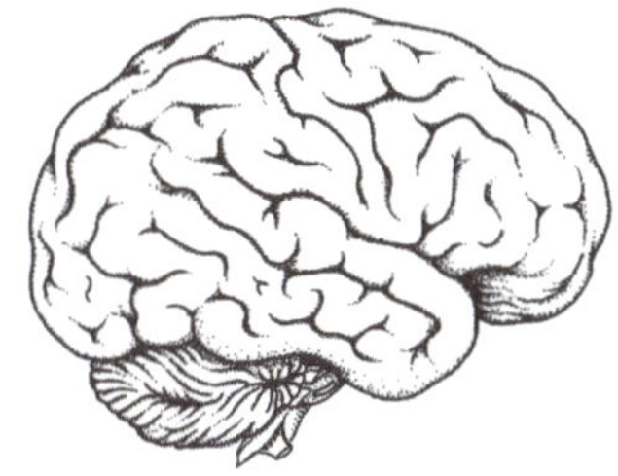

DO YOU LIE? DO YOU HURT? IF SO WHY? EXPLAIN THE LAST TIME YOU KNOWINGLY LIED OR HURT SOMEONE.

Eclectic: deriving ideas, style, or taste from a broad and diverse range of sources.

PSYCH/QUOTES

Passion and persistence turns pain into progress.

MY INNERSTANDING OFME

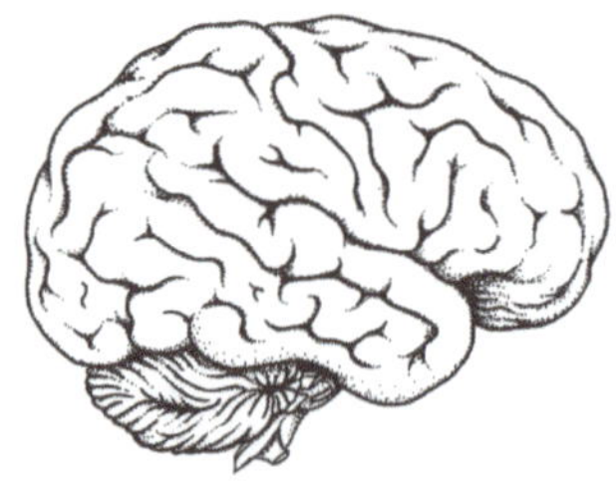

HOW DO YOU FEEL WHEN YOU HAVE TO TAKE RESPONSIBILITY FOR SOMETHING. BAD/GOOD. EXPLAIN WHY YOU THINK YOU FEEL THIS WAY.

Culture:
the customs, arts, social institutions, and achievements of a particular nation, people, or other social group.

NOTES

MY INNERSTANDING OFME

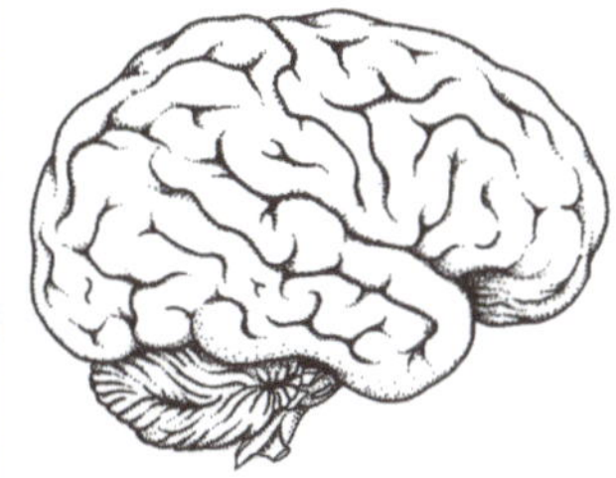

DO YOU HELP THOSE IN NEED? WHY SHOULD YOU? WHY SHOULDN'T YOU?(*PROS/CONS)

Essence: the intrinsic nature or indispensable quality of something.

PSYCH/QUOTES

The inner reality creates the outer form.

MY INNERSTANDING OFME

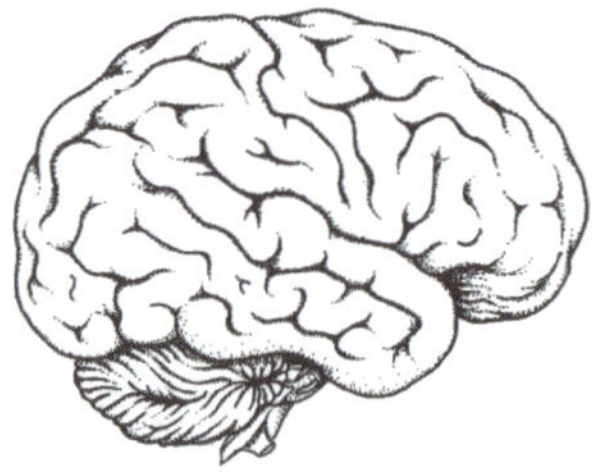

HOW DO YOU BELIEVE ONE SHOULD SHOW LOYALTY? WHAT DOES LOYALTY CONSIST OF? WHATS THE BEST REACTION TO BROKEN LOYALTY?

Propaganda: information, especially of a biased or misleading nature, used to promote or publicize a particular political cause or point of view.

NOTES

MY INNERSTANDING OF ME

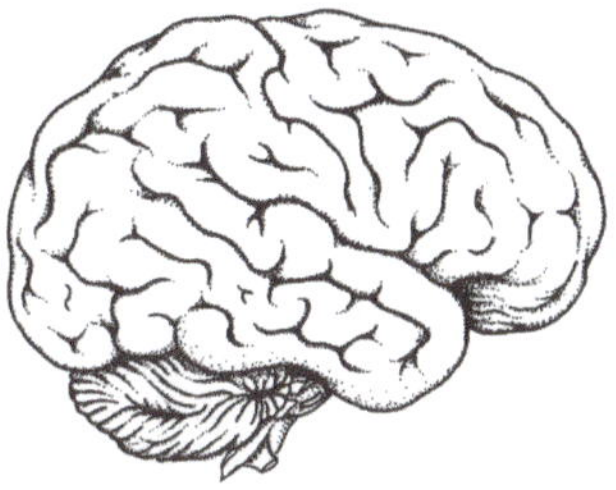

DO YOU FEEL MORE COMFORTABLE/CONFIDENT LEADING OR FOLLOWING? OR OTHER? WHY?

Ostentatious: a vulgar or pretentious display, designed to impress or attract attention.

NOTES

MY INNERSTANDING OFME

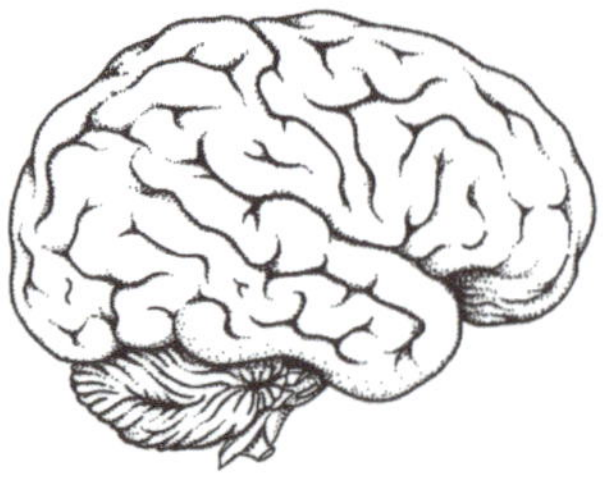

Pellucid: very well defined in meaning and style.

HOW WOULD YOU LIKE FOR PEOPLE TO RESPOND WHEN YOU'RE FEELING STRESSED? HAPPY?

PSYCH

A bad mood is never an excuse to use cruel words. Moods change but words can scar forever.

INTERACTIVE BUILDING ACTIVITY

ACTIVITY

ASK AN ELDER

What affect do you have or want to have on the people around you?

Have you ever helped someone else to get better at something in his or her life? How did you encourage that person?

Do you think the community is responsible for protecting its youth? How can we go about protecting them?

What are your beliefs on platonic relationships between the opposite sex? What makes a platonic relationship healthy?

Ask a close friend when was the last time they cried. What made them cry?

Pick up a pile of marbles and/or coins off the floor only using your toes, then place coins and marbles in a cup. How many can you pick up in a minute? Try with friends.

What personal activities bring you excitement? What group activities bring you excitement?

While laying down with your eyes closed. Envision yourself living in your purpose. Imagine working in your dream profession. Describe your vision.

SCENERIOS

During lunch, you walk into the bathroom and witness your friend being bullied by a group of older much larger kids. Your friend needs your help. What do you do to save your friend? How do you ease the situation and prevent future incidents?

LEVEL IV

L4-TASK CHALLENGE

What are your fighting disciplines? Which ones would you like to learn? Honestly rate yourself from 1-10 (*10 being mastery) in your ability to protect yourself without using a fire arm. What do you think is the best response after losing a fight?

How do you express love and affection? Describe the a time when you felt the most loved and appreciated? What brought on this feeling?

Create a yearly clothing/shoe budget for yourself and dependents.

MY INNERSTANDING OF ME

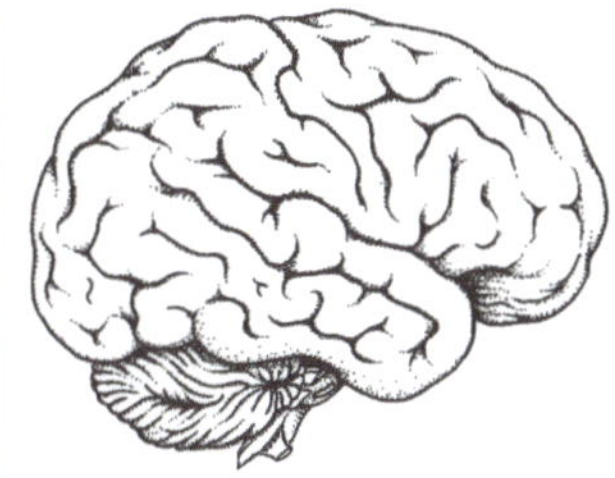

WHAT DO YOU BELIEVE WILL BE YOUR BIGGEST CHALLENGE IN THE FUTURE? HOW DO YOU PLAN TO OVERCOME IT?

Cognizance: knowledge, awareness, or notice.

PSYCH/QUOTES

Anything that you can do in 5 minutes, do it immediately. Don't wait!

MY INNERSTANDING OF ME

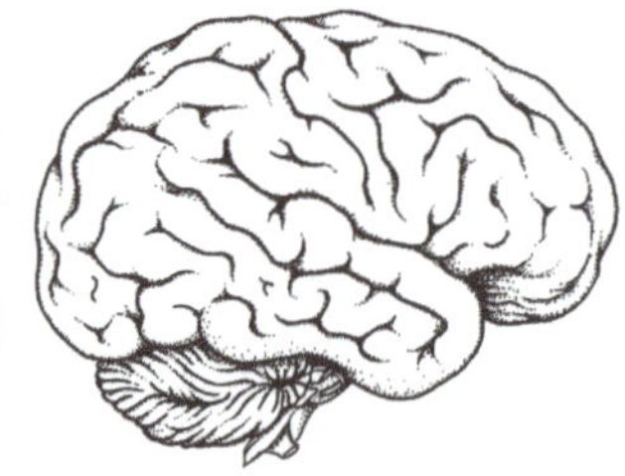

WHAT HAS BEEN YOUR BIGGEST TRIUMPH AND ACCOMPLISHMENT? WHAT WAS ITS SIGNIFICANCE?

Abuse:
use or treat in such a way as to cause damage or harm.

NOTES

MY INNERSTANDING OFME

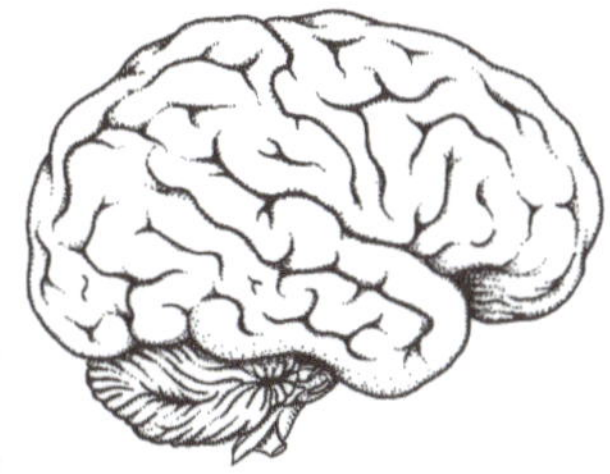

WHAT TYPE OF MOTIVATION BRINGS THE BEST OUT OF YOU? DESCRIBE AN INSTANCE THIS TYPE OF MOTIVATION WORKED FOR YOU.

Determinism: the doctrine that all events, including human action, are ultimately determined by causes external to the will.

PSYCH/QUOTES

When meeting someone new, make complete eye contact long enough to notice their eye color. Too much may be uncomfortable. The right amount builds respect.

MY INNERSTANDING OFME

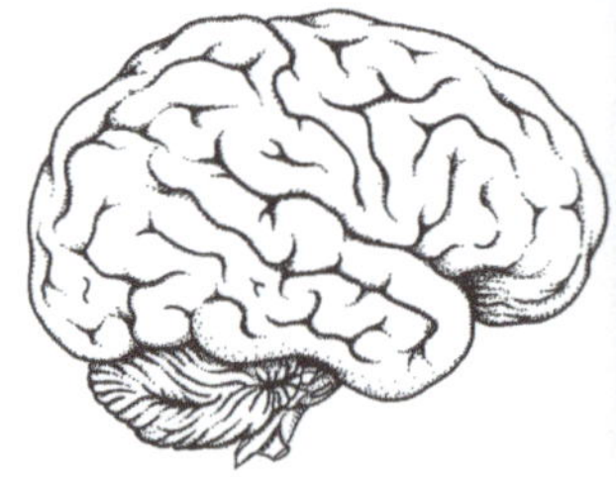

CURRENTLY, WHAT ARE YOUR TOP 3 PRIORITIES? WHY ARE THESE AT THE TOP?

Patience: the capacity to accept or tolerate delay, inconvenience, or suffering without getting angry or upset.

PSYCH/QUOTES

Learn from the past. Live in the present. Prepare for the future. Embrace the unknown.

MY INNERSTANDING OFME

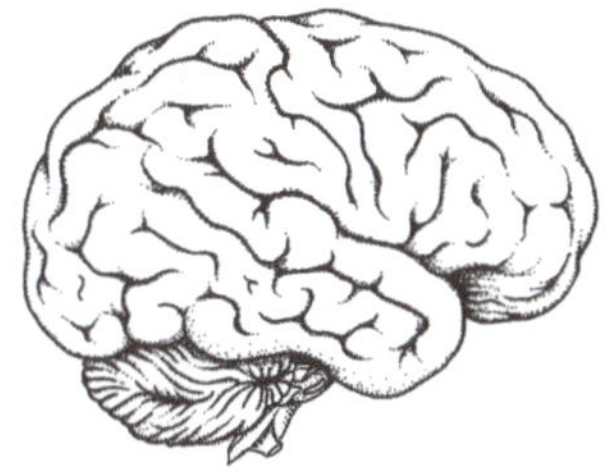

WHAT ARE SOMETHINGS YOU CAN INVEST IN NOW THAT COULD PREPARE YOU FOR THE FUTURE YOU DESIRE ?

Appropriation: the action of taking something from a person or group for one's own use, typically without the owner's permission

NOTES

MY INNERSTANDING OFME

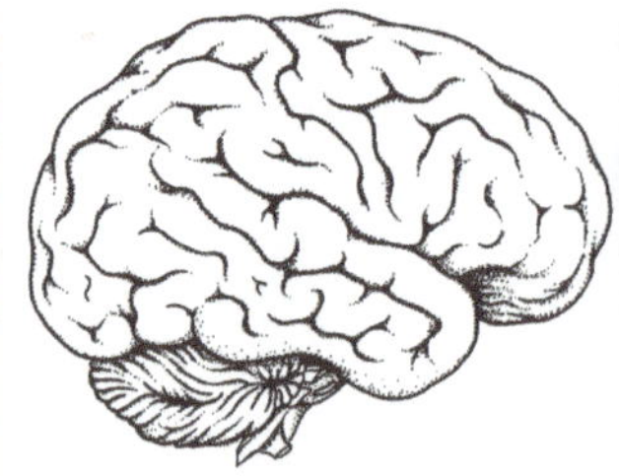

DESCRIBE IN DETAIL YOUR DREAM VACATION. WHAT WOULD IT TAKE TO GET THERE? HOW MUCH MONEY WOULD YOU NEED? WHO WOULD YOU TAKE?

Savant: a learned person, an intellectual scholar

PSYCH/QUOTES

Pay Attention to Intentions.

MY INNERSTANDING OF ME

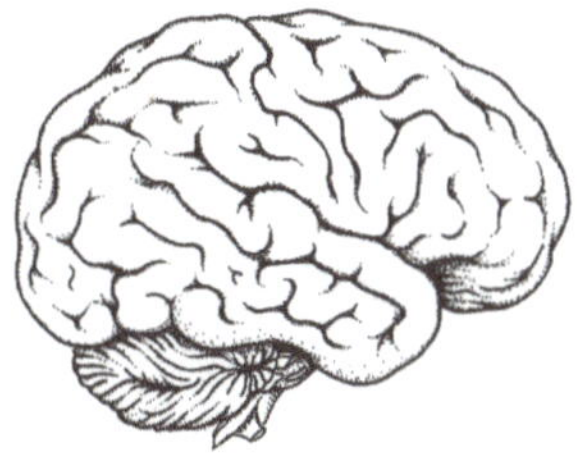

WHAT ARE SOMETHINGS YOU WANT TO KNOW/LEARN/MASTER IN THE NEXT 5 YEARS? 10 YEARS?

Collective: a group of individuals working together to accomplish a task or mission.

Are you part of any collectives or groups? Which collective or group has your respect? Why?

NOTES

MY INNERSTANDING OFME

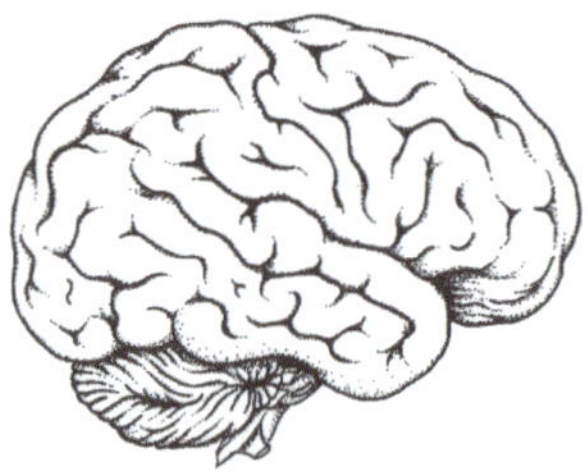

WHAT ARE SOME THINGS THAT YOU'RE THANKFUL FOR?

Prolific: producing much fruit or foliage

PSYCH/QUOTES

Motivate yourself from within.

MY INNERSTANDING OFME

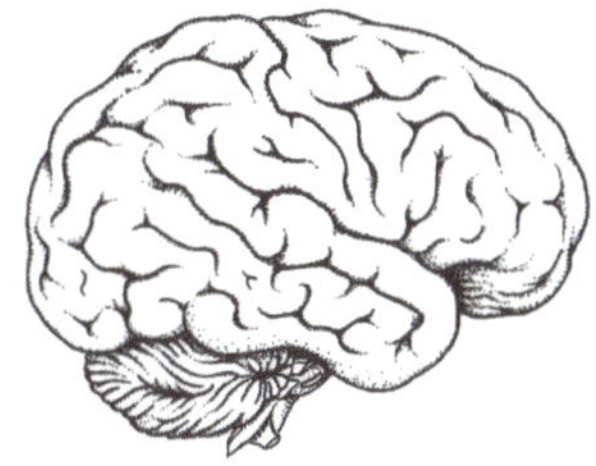

Asset:
a useful or valuable thing, person, or quality

DO YOU FEEL LIKE YOUR PEERS ARE UNDER STRESS? HOW CAN YOU TELL? HOW SHOULD YOU RESPOND?

PSYCH/QUOTES

Put out the same energy you would like to receive.

MY INNERSTANDING OFME

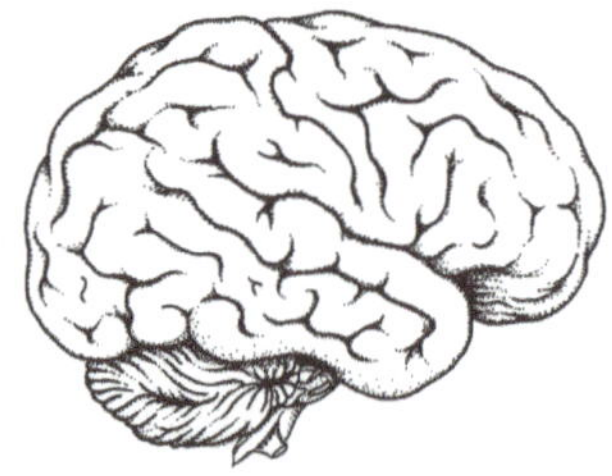

HOW CAN YOU SERVE OTHERS?

Optimist: one who tends to be hopeful and confident about the future or the success of something.

PSYCH/QUOTES

An angry heart will eventually devour its owner.

INTERACTIVE BUILDING ACTIVITY

ACTIVITY

Draw a picture of an object in front of you, without looking down at the pencil or paper. Don't look down! Try with friends.

Create a calendar for the next 3 months. Keep it updated with all of your activities.

List the people around you that inspire and motivate you to be better.

When discussing a serious topic, use a round table format, instead of an argument/debate format.

Today, introduce yourself to someone you always wanted to meet and get to know.

SCENERIOS

During a project, you're grouped with a person you do not like. How do you respond?

ASK AN ELDER

Currently, what are your top 5 priorities?

Describe your perfect day.

What is leadership? What qualities should a great leader possess?

What are 3 things you wish you would've practiced growing up, that would've put you in a better situation today?

Complete the Venn diagram by listing differences and similarities.

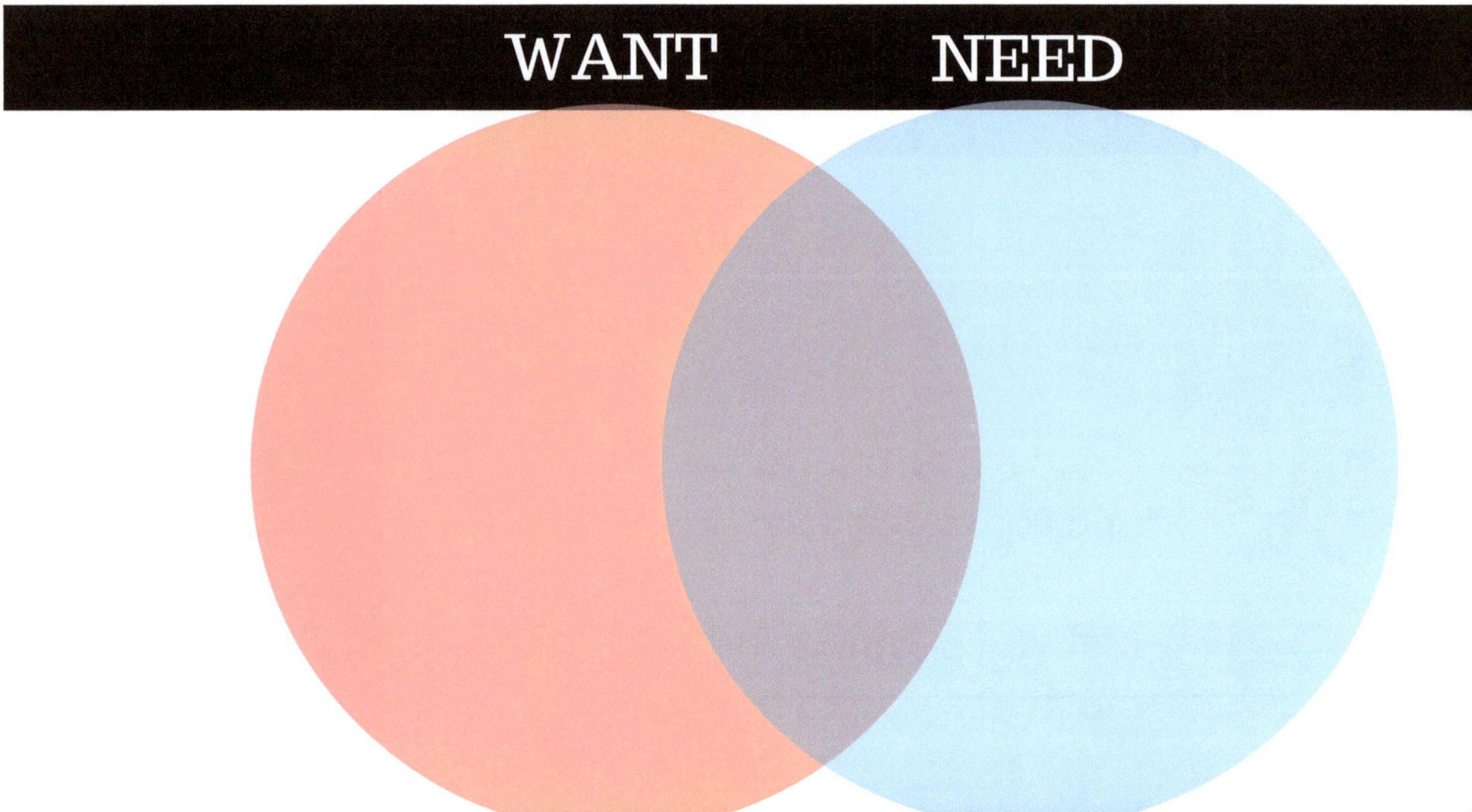

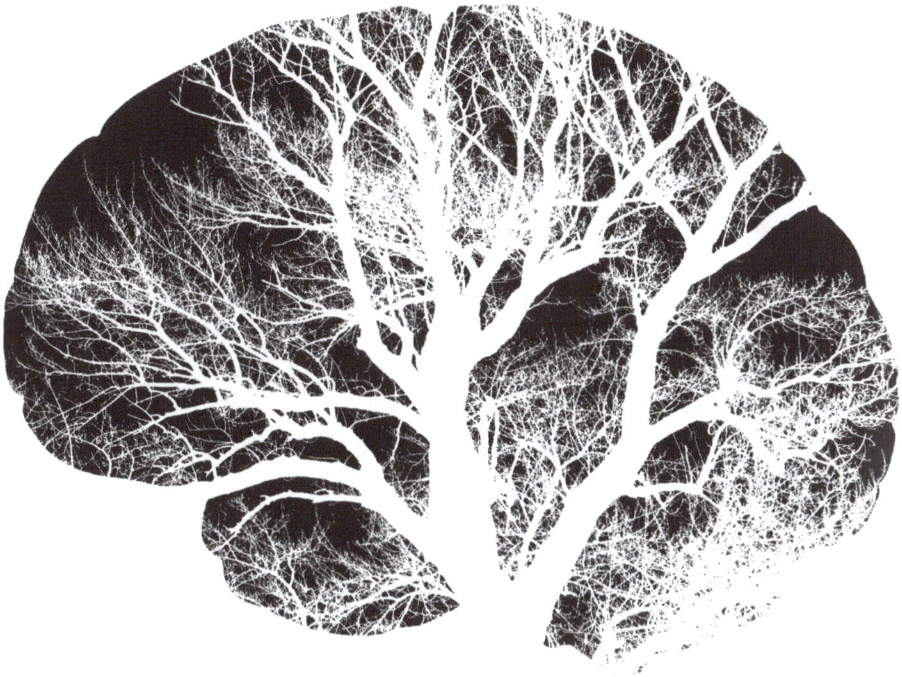

LEVEL V

L5-TASK CHALLENGE

Go back to a school you've attended and teach something valuable you've learned professionally or financially.

Smile whenever you enter a room and greet everyone with a smile.

Find 10 new words to learn every month. As you learn them, incorporate the words into your everyday language.

Why do you want to be successful and reach your goals? Write a why statement. It helps to give your actions purpose.

MY INNERSTANDING OFME

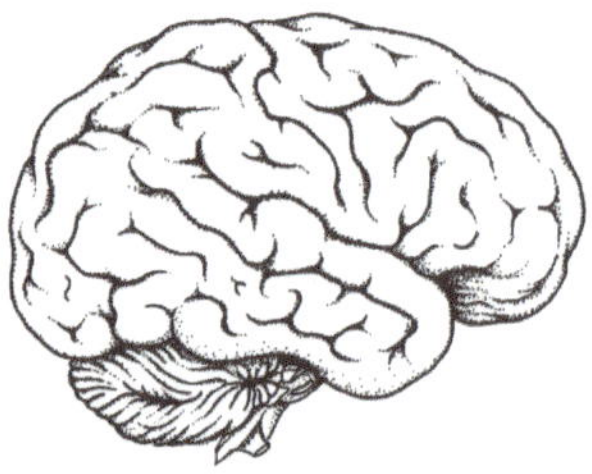

WRITE DOWN HOW YOU WANT YOUR DAILY LIFE TO BE. HOW DO YOU WANT TO LIVE? BE ABSOLUTE.

Tradition: a long-established custom or belief that has been passed on from one generation to another

PSYCH/QUOTES

Assumptions can be time consuming and costly in many ways. So always ask questions to gain full understanding of pertinent information.

MY INNERSTANDING OFME

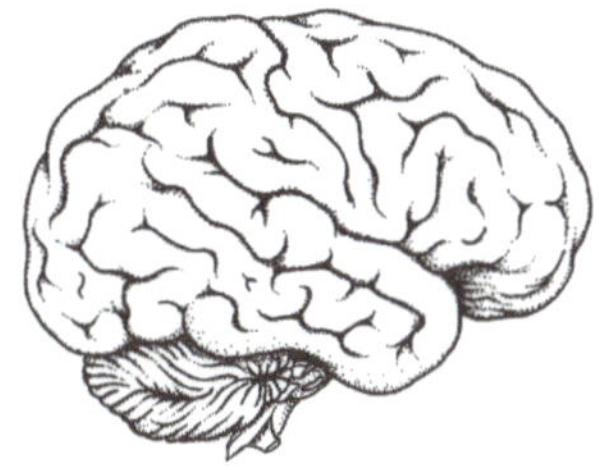

DESCRIBE YOUR STYLE WHEN IT COMES TO FASHION/ART?

Genius: exceptional intellectual or creative power or other natural ability.

NOTES

MY INNERSTANDING OFME

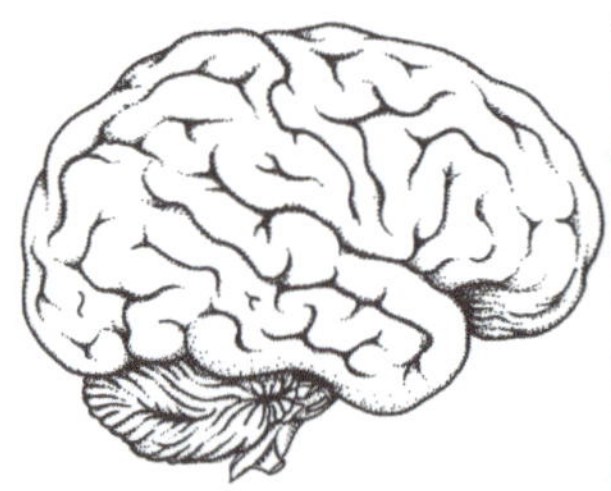

WHAT MAKES YOU HAPPY?

Defeatist: one who expects or is excessively ready to accept failure.

PSYCH/QUOTES

Comparison is the cancer of happiness.

MY INNERSTANDING OFME

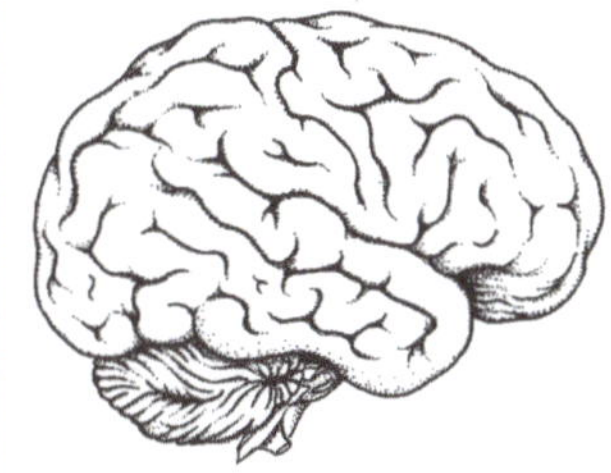

WHAT TYPE OF PERSON DO YOU WANT TO BE WHEN FACED WITH ADVERSITY? HOW DO YOU REACT NOW?

Moral:
the principles of right & wrong behavior and the goodness or badness of human character.

PSYCH/QUOTES

He who comes prepared can smile in the mist of war.

MY INNERSTANDING OFME

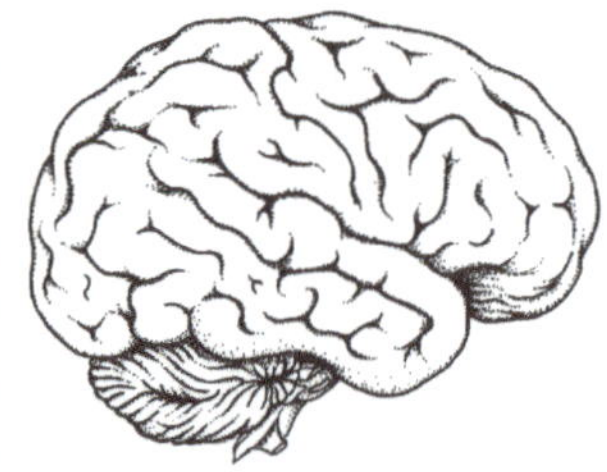

WHAT ARE THE THINGS THAT YOU WON'T DO? WHY?

Conscious: to be aware and have knowledge of something, or ones self, surroundings, environment.

PSYCH/QUOTES

Anything you study, do repeatedly and consistently you will eventually master.

MY INNERSTANDING OF ME

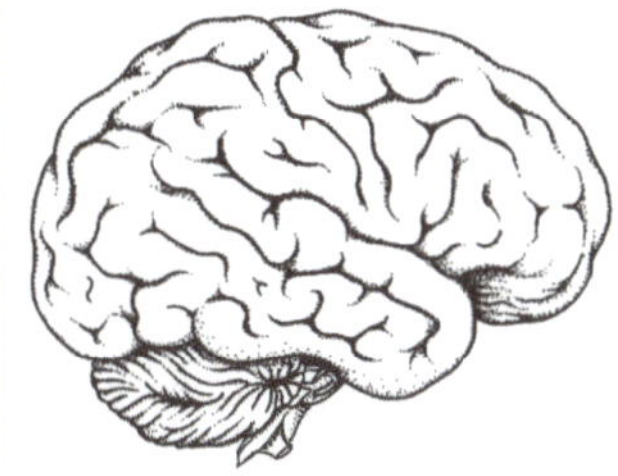

WHAT THINGS ARE MOST IMPORTANT TO YOU?

Grit: courage and resolve; strength of character.

NOTES

MY INNERSTANDING OFME

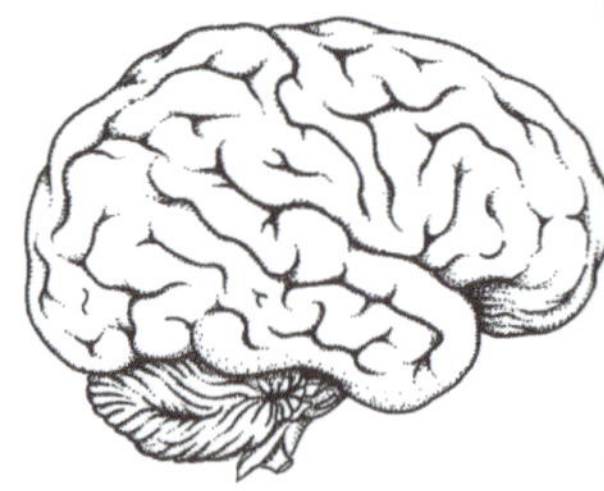

Righteous: the quality of being morally right or justifiable.

DO YOU LIKE WHO YOU'RE BECOMING? EXPLAIN.

PSYCH/QUOTES

Everything you need to be great is already within. You just have to want to find it.

MY INNERSTANDING OFME

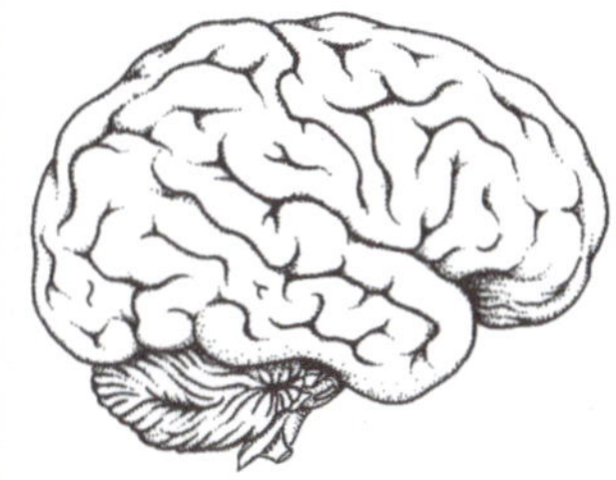

WHAT IS ONE AREA OF YOUR LIFE THAT YOU ALREADY EXCEL IN? WRITE ABOUT WHY YOU ARE SO GOOD AT THAT ONE PARTICULAR THING AND HOW YOU CAN CONTINUE TO SUCCEED IN THAT AREA OF YOUR LIFE?

Vigor: physical strength and good health

PSYCH/QUOTES

Surround yourself with thinkers, innovators and doers who discuss ideas, progression, and solutions not those who gossip about people.

MY INNERSTANDING OFME

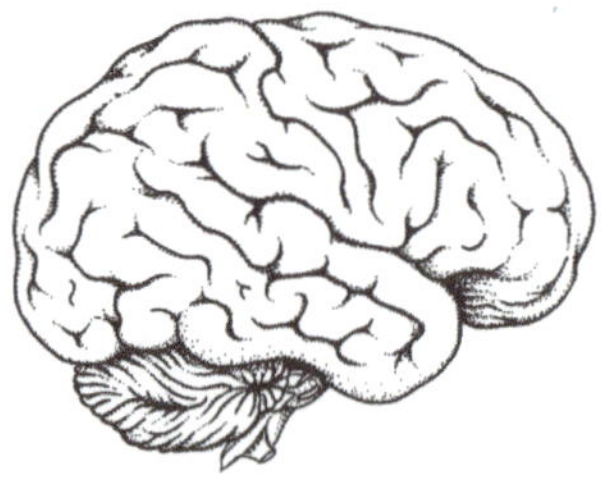

WHAT ARE SOMETHINGS YOUR PEERS HAVE CONVINCED YOU TO DO THAT WERE BAD, IN WHICH YOU WOULD NOT HAVE DONE ALONE? WHAT ARE SOME GOOD THINGS? WHY DID YOU DO IT?

Self Governance: having control or rule over oneself and actions, specially. Living by a set of laws set by oneself.

PSYCH/QUOTES

Remind yourself often of your blessings. Don't allow them to stop your pursuit to your desired goal.

INTERACTIVE BUILDING ACTIVITY

ACTIVITY

Tell 2 truths about yourself to a friend.

List your top 3 favorite music artists. Then give 3 reasons why you like their music. Next describe in detail how their music makes you feel when you listen to it.

Write a letter to your younger self informing you of something you wish you knew when you were younger. How has the information helped you in present day?

Create a list of 10 people who are successful in the profession you want to enter. How did they get there? Write down questions to ask them that you believe will help you in your journey to success.

Listen to music and try to figure out all of the instruments being played.

ASK AN ELDER

Describe what karma means to you?

What is the greatest lesson you've learned in relation to personal growth? Why is it so important to you?

How much is an hour of your life worth?

SCENERIOS

Your friend borrows money from you for a project their doing. The friend is unable to pay you back in time and wont have the money for another month or so. How do you respond to their shortcomings? A month passes and your friend still doesn't have the money. It's looking like you're never going to get your money back. How would you feel? How would you respond?

Complete the Venn diagram highlighting and explaining the differences and similarities

Settling Contentment

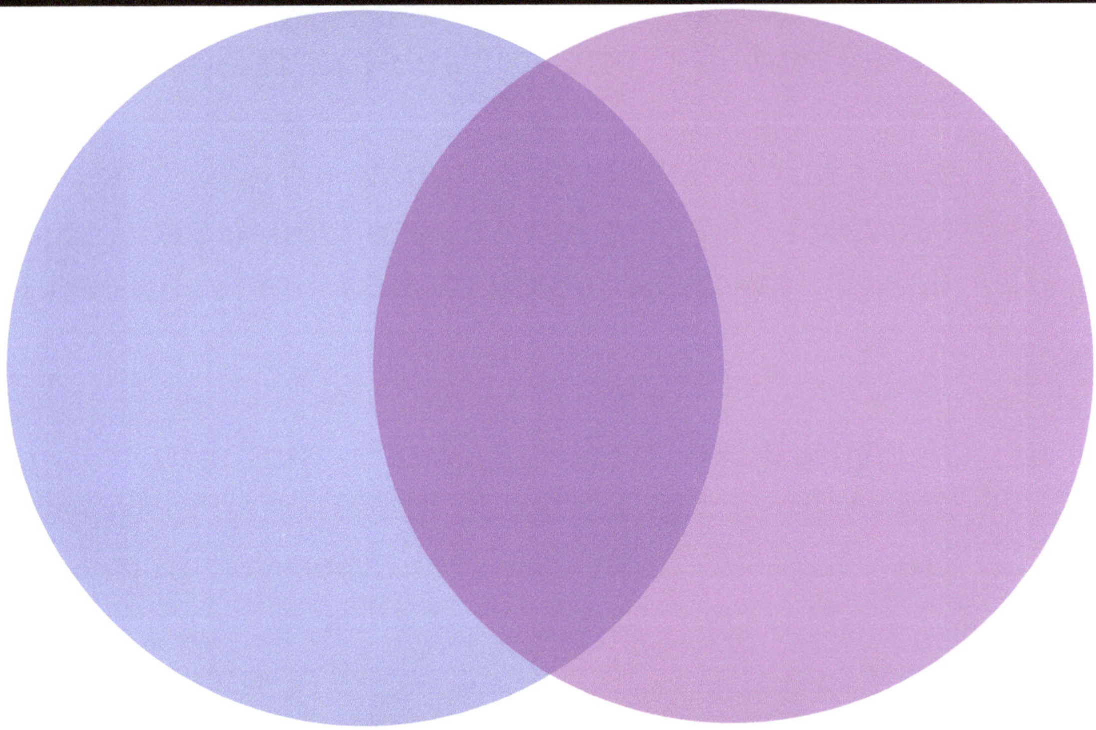

Confidence Arrogance

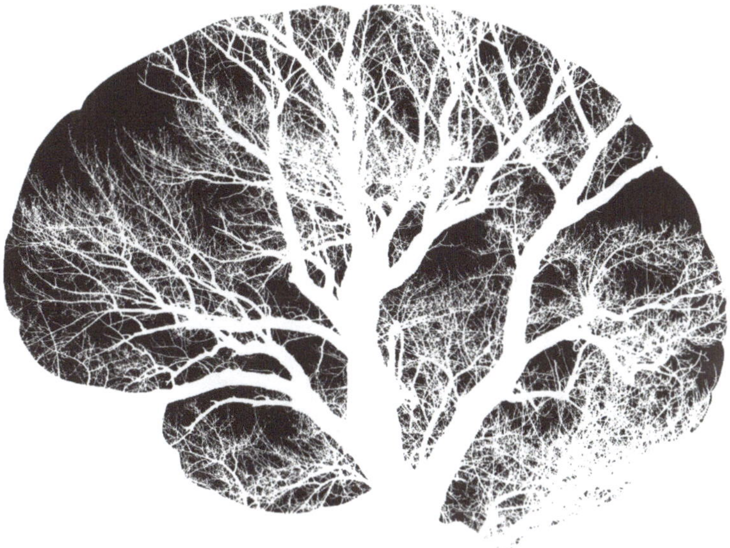

LEVEL VI

L6-TASK CHALLENGE

Give 3 thoughtful compliments a day for a week. At the end of the week, write down how it made you feel. How do you think it made others feel?

Forgive a debt that you've been owed.

How often do you read? Where do you receive most of your reading material? (Social media, books, newspapers, etc.) How many words can you read a minute? Time yourself.

10 GET YOUR 10 IN!

Choose one or a mix to do every month for a year

- Donate $10 a month to an organization
- Give 10 hours of community service a month
- Exercise for 10 hours a month
- Do 10 good deeds a month
- Pick up 10 items of trash on your street a day for a month
- Within a month, go to 10 new places, & meet 10 different people
- Recruit 10 new people a month to commit to the challenge

MY INNERSTANDING OFME

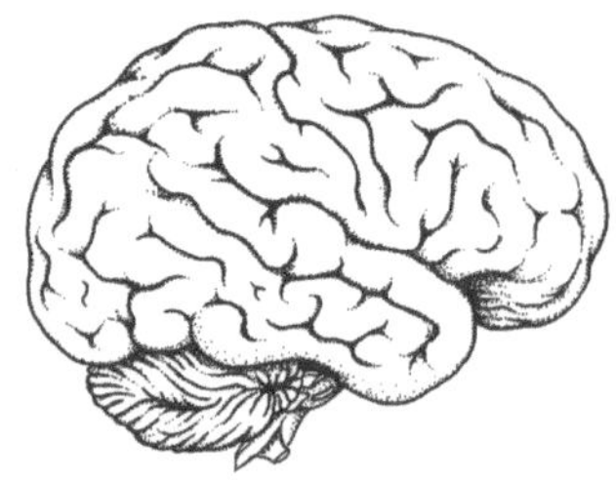

WHAT CHARACTERISTICS DO YOU WANT TO BE KNOWN FOR?

Utopia:
a place or state of things in which everything is perfect, according to ones own standards.

Describe your idea of a utopia, and what it would consist of.

PSYCH/QUOTES

Don't be fearful of the results of being and doing your best.

MY INNERSTANDING OF ME

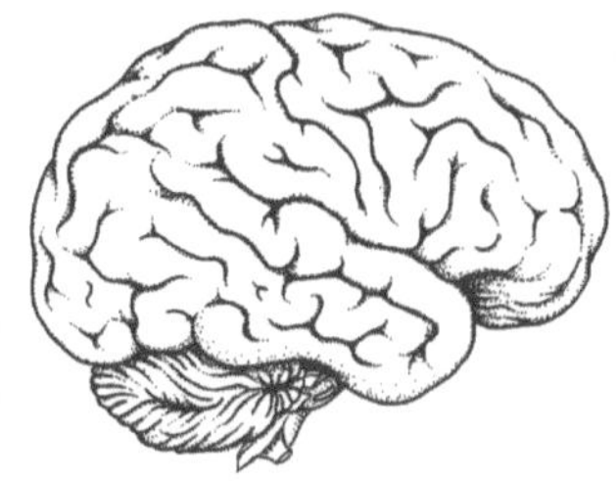

Concise:
giving a lot of information clearly and in a few words; brief but comprehensive.

TO DATE, WHAT HAS BEEN YOUR BIGGEST CHALLENGE? HOW DID YOU OVERCOME IT? WOULD YOUR APPROACH FOR THAT CHALLENGE BE THE SAME IF IT HAPPENED TODAY?

PSYCH/QUOTES

Your goals should be specific, measurable, attainable, realistic, and time-bound. Just add enthusiasm and resilience. Work S.M.A.R.T.E.R not harder.

MY INNERSTANDING OFME

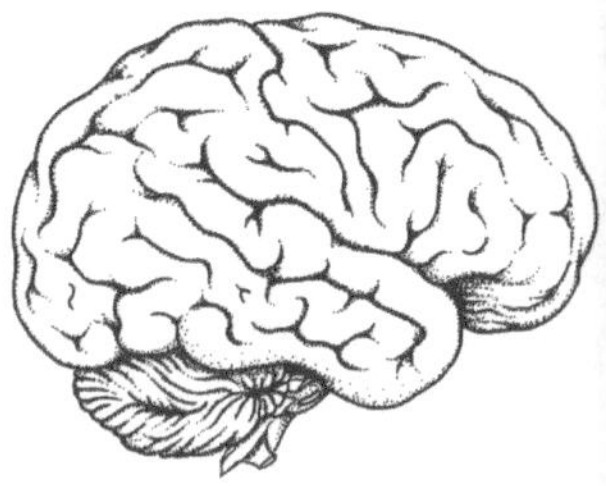

WHAT DO YOU BELIEVE IN? RELIGION? SPIRITUAL? WHY? WHO TAUGHT YOU? WHO TAUGHT THEM? DO YOU ACTIVELY PRACTICE YOUR BELIEFS? DO YOUR BELIEFS CAUSE YOU TO HELP, OR HURT OTHERS?

Priorities: something that is regarded, acted on, and treated as more important than another.

PSYCH/QUOTES

Train your brain and heart to be your best ally, not your biggest liability.

MY INNERSTANDING OFME

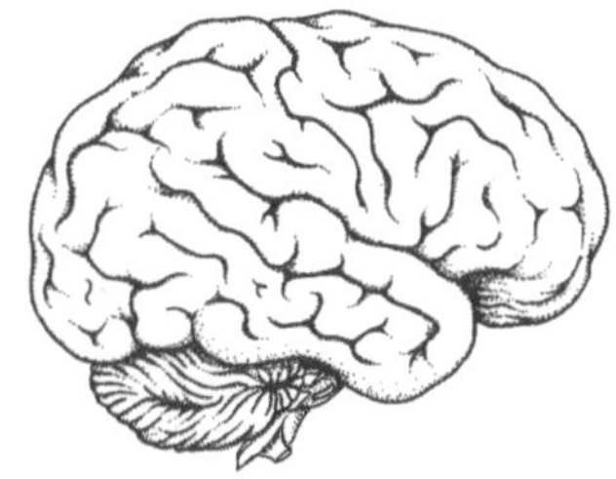

HOW DO YOU COMMUNICATE WHEN YOU"RE HURT OR ANGRY? IS IT HEALTHY FOR YOU AND THOSE AROUND YOU?

Dogma:
is an official system of principles or doctrines, laid down by an authority as incontrovertibly true

NOTES

MY INNERSTANDING OFME

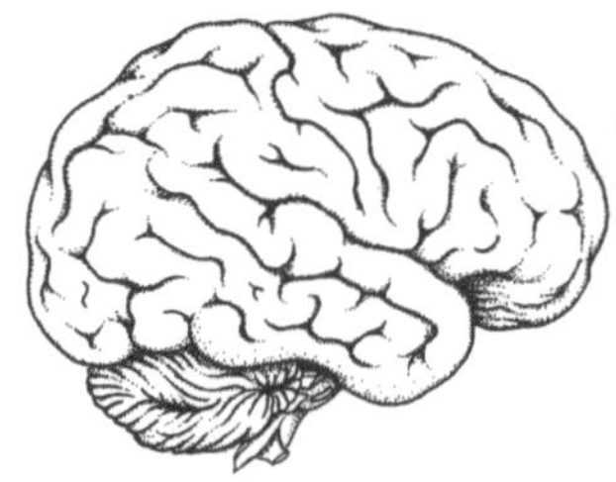

WHAT DOES SEX MEAN TO YOU? WHAT IS IT? WHAT DOES IT INVOLVE? WHY IS IT IMPORTANT TO CHOOSE PARTNERS WISELY? WHAT ARE YOUR REQUIREMENTS BEFORE BECOMING INTIMATE WITH SOMEONE?

Economics: knowledge concerned with the production, consumptio n, and transfer of wealth.

PSYCH/QUOTES

Hard work and determination are the steroids for your talents and skills.

MY INNERSTANDING OFME

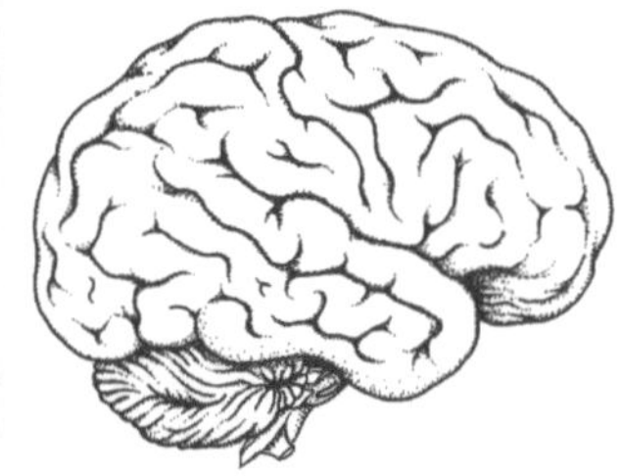

WHAT IS YOUR BIGGEST FEAR? WHAT OTHER SMALL FEARS DO YOU HAVE? ARE THEY STOPPING YOU FROM EXCELING IN ANYWAY?

Self-efficacy: ones belief in their natural innate ability to achieve goals.

PSYCH/QUOTES

Pay attention to how your moral compass is being shaped by the people in your life.

MY INNERSTANDING OFME

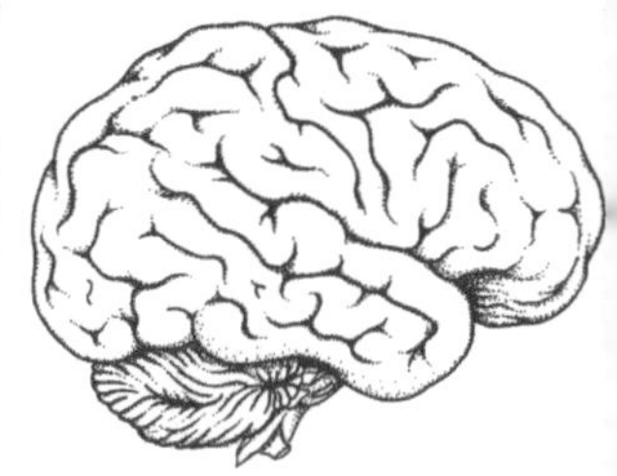

WHAT THINGS DO YOU BRING INTO A RELATIONSHIP? DO YOU HAVE ALL THAT YOU ASK FOR? WHAT ARE THE THINGS YOU WANT/NEED TO HAVE BEFORE ENTERING A RELATIONSHIP?

Passive: accepting or allowing what happens or what others do, without active response or resistance.

What are some good and bad times to be passive? Why?

PSYCH/QUOTES

Be solid, always uphold your morals and righteousness no matter the situation.

MY INNERSTANDING OFME

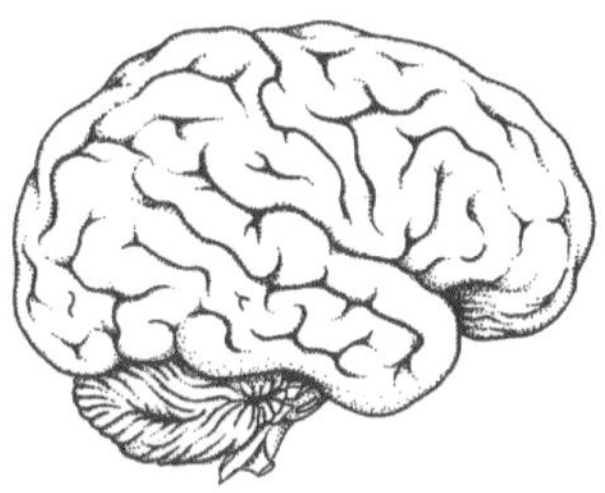

HOW DO YOU DEFINE PERSONAL GROWTH? AFTER DEFINING THE WORD, WRITE ABOUT WHY IT IS IMPORTANT FOR PEOPLE TO STRIVE TO IMPROVE THEMSELVES.

Influence:
The ability to have an effect on the character, development, or behavior of someone or something, or the effect itself

What are some things you have influence over? List some things that influence you to be better.

NOTES

MY INNERSTANDING OFME

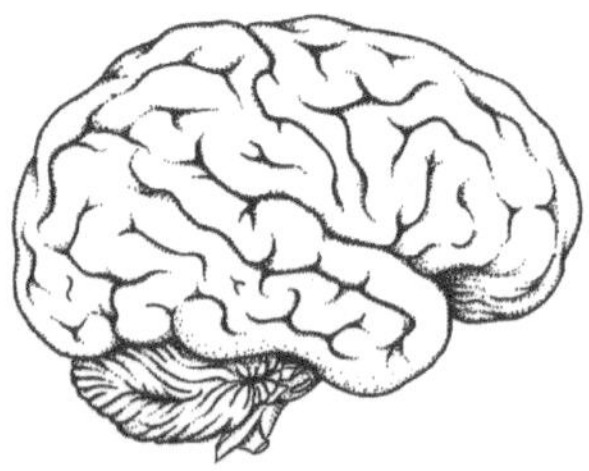

WHAT WOULD YOU DO IF YOU KNEW YOU COULD NOT FAIL? WHAT WOULD YOU DO WITH YOUR TIME AND MONEY WERE NO OBJECT?

Principle: a fundamental truth or proposition that serves as the foundation for a system of belief or behavior or for a chain of reasoning.

PSYCH/QUOTES

Believe in yourself and your ability to complete a task correctly, in a timely manner, with little to no supervision.

INTERACTIVE BUILDING ACTIVITY

ACTIVITY

ASK AN ELDER

/hat are some
ıings I should be
urrently be
ıvesting in? Do you
ave any financial
ps or advice?

/hat books do you
ave in your
ɔllection? Which
ɔok or books were
ıost helpful?

/hat is your
iggest fear?

/hat do you value?
/hat matters most
ɔ you?

escribe your
ıvorite memory.

/hat physical &
haracter traits
rouse you about
ıe opposite sex?

Write a speech, motivating a group of people to be strong, happy, and/or to complete a task. Recite it aloud.

Write a poem to your ideal mate.

When eating, try to identify individual ingredients in your meal, including subtle herbs and spices.

Make a list of 10 things that make you happy. How can you experience these things more frequently?

SCENERIOS

You see a person you're acquainted with steal a ring from a stranger and hides it. When asked,, they say you have it. Now the stranger is angry. What would you do? How would you respond? How does being blamed for something you didn't do make you feel?

You borrow money from a friend for a project and are unable to pay it back in time. You wont have it for a month. How do you go about telling the friend of your shortcomings without damaging the friendship?

Complete the Venn diagrams by listing differences and similarities.

FACT

ASSUMPTION/ OPINION

CONNECTION

ATTACHMENT

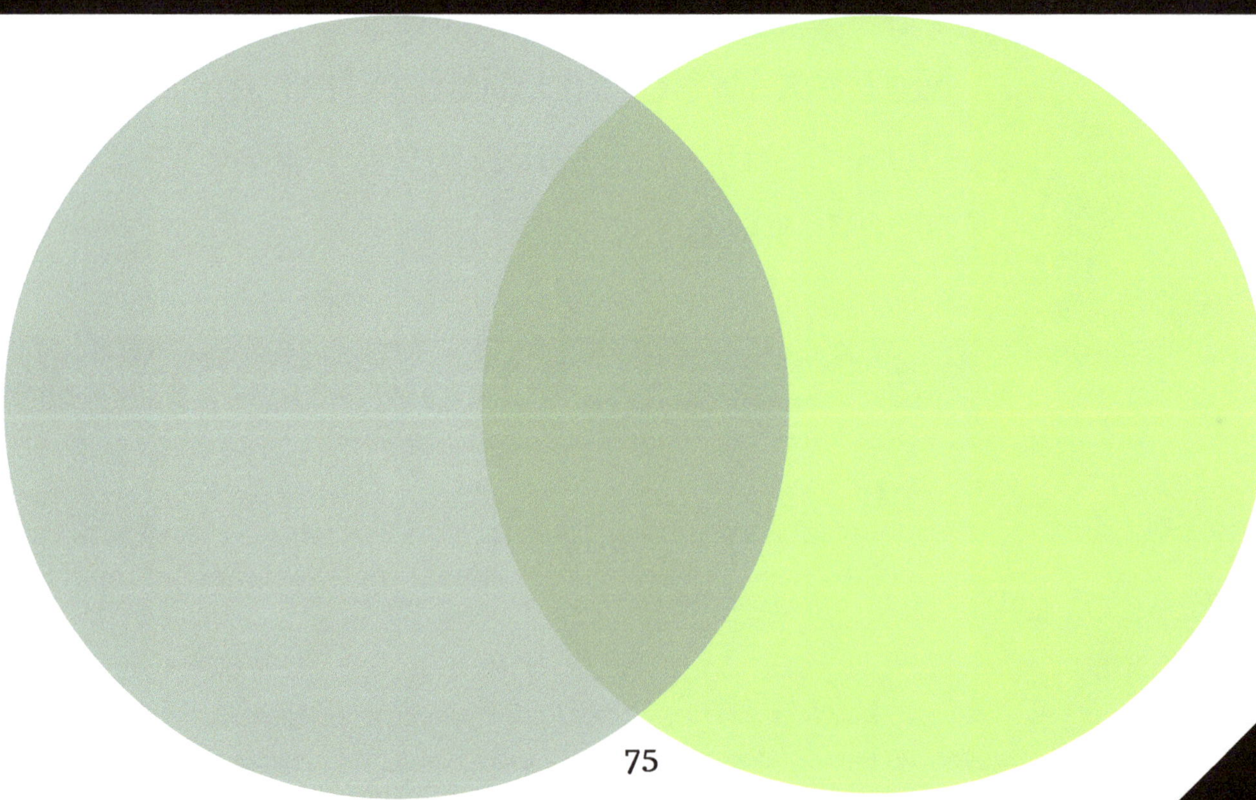

Accomplishments to date

Description	Date	Significance to you

Things You want to Accomplish

Description	Significance to you
☐	
☐	
☐	
☐	
☐	

Notes

References

https://www.pon.harvard.edu/daily/conflict-resolution/conflict-resolution-strategies/

https://www.edutopia.org/blog/8-pathways-why-resourcefulness-matters-marilyn-price-mitchell

www.ingramcontent.com/pod-product-compliance
Lightning Source LLC
LaVergne TN
LVHW071057210826
846010LV00055B/106
* 9 7 8 0 9 9 7 5 0 4 2 4 8 *